Kids who Kill:

ERIC SMITH

Book 2, Series 1

KATHRYN McMASTER

ISBN: 9788894122862

DEDICATION

To Derrick Robie, robbed of a life and taken far too soon.

CONTENTS

AUTHOR'S NOTE

The story of Derrick Robie's murder was reconstructed through actual events. The information given and the crime depicted is based on legal evidence, statements, eyewitness accounts, court transcripts, testimony given by those involved, personal interviews, individual research, and media resources.

ACKNOWLEDGMENTS

My thanks to the newspaper archives from which I was able to retrieve numerous articles and to the journalists who covered this story extensively. I am grateful too, for the court transcripts available for copy, albeit very few. Finally, a big thank you goes to my editor, Kathleen Lance, who is such an important asset in giving sage advice and in whom I trust implicitly, and the rest of my strong editorial team who are invaluable and indispensable.

Best Wishes!

Kathryn Mc Master.

1. SAVONA, NEW YORK

The sleepy pastoral village of Savona, settled in the 1700s, lies sixty miles southeast of Rochester in Steuben County NY. Shadowed by steep-sided hills, clad with lush vegetation and trees, the Cohocton River divides the settlement and Rattlesnake Hill, so named for its proliferation of the reptile, rises beyond the recreation fields and dominates Savona.

In 1993, with a population of 974, the village boasts maple-lined streets with one blinking red traffic light at the intersection of Routes 415 and 226, two gas stations, a hardware store, a grocery store and a diner. Five minutes of travel in any direction and you are into the countryside.

Over the years, Savona has not been without its share of tragedies. There is a murder-suicide, two teenagers killed by a drunk driver, a child tragically suffocates in a snowbank, and a tractor accident takes the life of a promising high school senior.

Nothing however can prepare them for the next tragedy that rocks their community on the morning of August 2, 1993. This tragedy will change their village forever.

A young boy murdered. A killer is at large. Fear infiltrates and seeps through the village, into the very sinew and bones of its inhabitants. Parents keep a closer eye on their children, buying them new whistles to hang around their necks, insisting they go out in groups if they cannot keep them off the streets. Padlocks fly off shop shelves and people buy additional hardware for increased security. They speak in hushed voices. Who could it be?

Thoughts veer to the nearby highways bypassing the area. Could it be someone traveling through? Had they taken the Savona off-ramp from Route 17 to prey on the village children? Was it a pedophile, a parolee, an outsider? The murder is too shocking for it to have been one of their own. Of this, the residents are certain.

After volunteers find four-year-old Derrick Robie's crushed and mutilated body, rumors swirl and spread; the boy was sexually molested. The horror grows. Village folk gossip in low voices in the booths at the Savona Diner, around kitchen tables, or over neighbors' fences, mentioning names of single men of the community and finger-point possible perpetrators.

The murderer is no pedophile. He is no parolee. He is no outsider. He is no adult.

Four years before this shocking event, while the unsuspecting residents of Savona were living their lives and going about their daily business, the blossoming mind of a young killer who indeed lives among them, was already at work laying the groundwork; planning ways to kill his neighbor's cat.

The killer's name is Eric Smith. He is a heavy smoker, smoking nearly a pack of cigarettes a day and fast developing a nicotine addiction. He has flashes of uncontrollable anger. He constantly has strong urges to hurt someone or something. When he plans to kill the cat, he is nine. When he kills Derrick Robie, he is thirteen.

2. ERIC SMITH

The Smith family lives on the other end of the village in West Lomoka Avenue. The road stretches like a long finger away from the business center. There they live in a two-storey gray house with peeling trim and an old washtub decorating the street-facing porch. Christmas lights strung across the front façade are still up long after Easter. It is here thirteen-year-old Eric Smith lives with his mother Tammy, his stepfather Theodore 'Ted' Smith, his fifteen-year-old sister Stacy, and twelve-year-old stepsister Holly.

The Wilsons are a prominent local family. Tammy Smith was born a Wilson, and her grandfather, Carl Peters is a retired deputy sheriff. Eric's kinfolk are numerous. With four generations living nearby and with twenty-eight cousins, virtually everyone in Savona is acquainted with the Robies, the Wilsons, or both.

Ted Smith, is a mechanic and works for the Philips Lightning Co. plant in Bath. Tammy is a stay-at-home mom active in the community, especially with softball. In '93, she is the president of the Savona Cinderella Softball League. The rest of the family is also involved in the sport. Ted is a coach and her two daughters are players.

Ted Smith is Tammy's second husband. Her first

was Randy Hevner. Tammy and Randy are high school sweethearts when they marry in 1978. The couple is young; Randy is eighteen, Tammy a little younger, and their daughter Stacy arrives shortly afterwards. About a year later, in 1979, the couple separate, around the same time Eric is conceived. He is born January 22, 1980.

Eric is a toddler when Tammy takes Randy to court for lack of child support payments. Randy contests the paternity for soon after their divorce, Tammy, still pregnant with Eric, marries Ted Smith. After a series of tests medical results confirm Hevner is wrong. Eric is his. The debate of money owed dissipates when Randy Hevner allows Ted to adopt his son. Ted and Tammy Smith later complete their family with the birth of their daughter, Holly.

Tammy does not have an easy pregnancy with Eric and takes medication throughout each trimester. She is an epileptic and has been taking Trimethadione since the age of five. She continues using the drug while pregnant with all three children. Besides taking Trimethadione (Tridione), a medication known to cause fetal damage and largely discontinued in the 1960s, she takes Mebaral for depression.

By the time Eric is twenty-eight-months-old, a pediatrician describes him as "a child who is stubborn and who has temper tantrums at least daily". From the age of two until three-and-a-half, Eric engages frequently in head banging and holding his breath. He has speech problems and does not reach his milestones of walking or talking until after the age of two.

By the age of four he is thinking of girls.

By the time he is nine he is a heavy smoker.

Eric displays the 'triad' of symptoms some health professionals believe foretell later violence. He wets his bed until aged eleven, he is fascinated with fire, and he kills small animals.

At three years old he gets up during the night and sets a pile of papers alight on top of the kitchen stove in the trailer home where they are living.

Around the time he kills Archie LeBaron's cat, his parents reveal, he takes a playing card, lights it, and starts screaming when it melts onto his hand when he cannot remove it.

He takes a perverse pleasure in killing snakes with stones and torturing small creatures such as cats, mice, rabbits and birds. He drowns them or runs over cats with a four-wheeler. We hear from Ted that his son enjoys gutting the animals they have hunted.

Academically, Eric is behind his peers. After finally learning how to speak, he still has a speech defect that needs a therapist. He drools when he speaks and he continues to do this until he is eight or nine years old.

His teachers keep him back at school during the first and fifth grades due to his learning difficulties. By the time he is thirteen, he is only in the fifth grade, the same grade as his younger sister. These learning difficulties are diagnosed as "difficulties with recalling information he hears and remaining on task in the classroom". They are deemed "not severe enough to warrant special education placement".

Because Eric is not placed in special education, he makes little progress. His level of functionality at thirteen is of a third or fourth-grader. These delays have an impact on his self-esteem. When questioned at home about something, he often retorts, "I don't know, I guess I'm just stupid."

Eric's teachers do not see him as stupid. They see him as a bright underachiever. They also see him as something of an enigma. He can be both cocky and shy, the bully or a sweetheart. His moods are mercurial. However, his behavior at school is never such that he ends up in the principal's office.

He loves to read but not always books age-appropriate. He takes books out of the library seen by some as 'weird and morbid', like Christopher Pike's paperback mysteries depicting bloody violence directed at, and by, kids. He also avidly reads Stephen King novels with themes of murder, violence against children, pets, and abuse.

He enjoys music. He is crazy about country singer Garth Brooks and listens repeatedly to his tapes. As a member of the school band he plays the trombone but is also learning to play the drums, something fast becoming a passion. He tells people when he grows up he wants to be a drummer. His dream is to play in a country-western band.

He tries hard to fit in with his peers by playing a number of sports. He likes to play soccer and football, basketball and baseball. He hangs out at the village park and sips soda pop in front of King's Groceries like most kids in the community.

The few who mingle with Eric say he likes Beavis and Butthead, an adult animated cartoon series on MTV that encourages anti-social behavior. The characters are dumb, crude, profane, and self-destructive. His friends recall his mimicry of the trademark Beavis and Butthead cackling laugh at any outrageous act, "Heh, heh, heh, that's cool". In juxtaposition, he also enjoys playing with G.I. Joe dolls.

He has a few friends, but not many, especially when growing up into an awkward teen. However, his attitude to most people is genial. He likes to make people laugh, takes on the role of class clown, and tells jokes. He also enjoys charming older girls and women.

Eric's learning problems and impulsivity are further compounded by his looks. He has a fiery thatch of red hair, a mask of copper freckles, and poor eyesight requiring him to wear thick lenses. Completing the picture is an unfortunate pair of low-set slightly deformed ears folding over at the top.

People remember him for his glasses. They are gold wire-rimmed aviators held together with a clump of tape at the bridge, swamping his small face.

Already his pale face shows anger towards the world at large. The narrow mouth is firmly set in a hard line, corners down-turned; a face etched in discontent. Yet the face is still that of a child's, much younger than his years, a face that still has not lost its baby fat.

His physical appearance and puny undersized frame weighing eighty pounds, a fiery temper, and frequent crying when put under duress, attract the bullies at his local school who set upon him mercilessly. Almost daily they mock his ears, his bright red hair, and go out of their way to trip him on the bus.

Eric relays he is often angry and wants to hurt someone. He is tired of the children picking on him, calling him names regarding his hair—'red hot, chili peppers', and worse. His sister remembers the bullying and an incident when a fellow pupil takes his school bag, empties the contents onto the floor, and then orders Eric to repack it. Taking the school bus becomes an ordeal he dreads.

The bullying makes him depressed, and he cries regularly. He tells his family, "I'm never going to be anybody."

One school year, after receiving his class photo, Eric scratches out his face on the photograph, telling his sister he is not "good enough" to be included.

Eric has never been told Ted adopted him as a baby. The revelation comes as a shock to the young boy when a classmate divulges the secret when he is nine. The boy taunts him about not knowing who his father is.

Ted Smith comes home from work late one night and finds Eric crying in the living room. After a little prodding Eric says he knows Ted is not his biological father. Ted sits with him and discusses the meaning of fatherhood. As he does so, Eric appears to understand that because Ted took care of him, loved him, and was with him during his time growing up, this makes Ted his father. Eric does not understand, however, why another child would tease him about it.

Eric is familiar with Randy, the man who is his biological father, and he sees him on many an occasion. However, Eric knows him as Stacy's father, not his own. Randy has remained close to Stacy after divorcing her mother, and has his daughter stay with him over weekends and vacations, but has never acknowledged Eric as his own, nor has he had him over to stay.

Once Eric starts putting the pieces together, he is overwhelmed with feelings of rejection. He would later say of his biological father, "He never really wanted me."

Ted Smith tries to be a decent father, but he often lashes out at Eric and is ill-equipped to give him any effective advice against bullying. Even his own mother tells him to try to ignore it. Ted readily admits he has a hot temper when it comes to Eric and the other children and tells them regularly he will "kick their butts up over their shoulders", or "I'm sick and tired of you", and "I'm sick of your crap."

In addition to the verbal abuse, Ted Smith is not averse to mete out physical punishment to the children either, including to "swat them upside the head." Many in the community feel the strapping six-footer Ted deals Eric a lot more beatings than he admits.

Marlene Heskell is a family friend of the Smiths. She and her husband John, meet Tammy and Ted Smith through Savona's Cinderella Softball program. Anna Heskell, her eleven-year-old daughter, participates alongside Holly Smith. From there the friendship grows and the two families often have dinner together and play cards.

Marlene and John, although reluctant to talk about the family, finally say Marlene once saw Smith lift Eric off the ground by his arm and kick him in the behind.

"And I saw him do it to other people's kids, too. A lot of people around here are afraid of Ted." Including she feels, Tammy Smith, a petite woman whose husband towers above her.

Another family friend adds Tammy "was afraid of Ted, but afraid to be without Ted as well. All her life she's had someone to take care of her."

Over and above the physical abuse there is also sexual abuse taking place within the home. Ted's stepdaughter Stacy is the victim. At the age of sixteen, she reveals Ted Smith sexually molested her when she was eleven, and again, at fourteen.

During the hearing we learn Ted is the son of alcoholic parents, who too was once abused by a relative. Ted and Tammy Smith admit to one occasion when he inappropriately fondles Stacy's breasts. Ted is forced out of the family home for a week and receives psychotherapy for his misconduct. The family goes to group counseling.

On a parental visiting weekend with Randy Hevner, Stacy tells her father she no longer wants to go back home, but wishes to live with him instead. He agrees and Stacy moves out of the Smith home in

May of '93 and resides with her biological father in the next town over. Stacy later says she feels guilty for not speaking out to the authorities about the issues that were taking place in the home.

Eric denies Ted Smith ever sexually abused him. At the same time, he denies Ted ever physically abused him. However, we know from eyewitness accounts, and by Ted's own admission, he is both physically and mentally abusive towards Eric.

Although Eric has difficulty in making friends and finding acceptance with his peers at school, he relates better to adults who view him as an agreeable, polite young man. He often shovels driveways for people, carries their shopping for them, or offers to take out their garbage. He is friendly, even affectionate. He craves attention and the love seemingly missing from his home environment.

"Eric liked to have someone put their arm around him, or talk nice to him," recalls Archie LeBaron, his next-door neighbor.

He particularly enjoys spending time with his grandparents, Red and Edie Wilson. Red says, "He'd always come in and give us hugs and kisses. He also liked being a clown."

Eric is no angel. He rams used apples and bananas into the exhaust pipes of cars whose owners are mean to him. He once threatens a teacher who had reprimanded him with, "You're dead."

Others see him differently.

"He was a very polite kid," says Laurie Elliott, who owns the Savona Diner with her husband Roy. Thirteen-year-old Eric plays with her ten-year-old son Bradley and she regularly has him over to dinner. He often asks her and other families if he can sleep over.

"I gave him extra treatment. I felt like he didn't have friends," she says. She goes on to say the boy often worried about whether girls liked him.

In June, during one of the girls' softball games, his friend Bradley Elliott prods Eric to talk to some young female players. He soon returns and expresses the girls don't like him because he is ugly. Laurie reassures him this is not true and that things will change once he is older.

She continues, "He'd always smile. One time he cleaned the house after I gave him some ice cream. There was no toughness about him."

Laurie Elliot and her husband Roy take Bradley and Eric on a Memorial Day vacation to Dorney Park in Allentown, Pa. The kids play and ride their bikes together. When they buy Eric a Harley Davidson T-shirt, he wears it for a week straight.

Roy Elliott does not feel the same way about Eric as his wife does. "I never liked the kid. He was a nice kid and all, but I was always suspicious of him. I don't know why. I just didn't trust him."

In personal communication with this author, John di Crasto tells of his first encounter with Eric. He says he went home afterwards and told his wife at the time, "I've just met the Anti-Christ."

When asked to explain the meaning of his comment, he explains he first met young Eric at a coffee klatch made up of private business owners, mechanics, welders, and CB operators.

"When Ted introduced his son to our group, Ted put his arm around him and embraced him. Eric had no emotion, just a stare. His eyes were cold and empty. It gave me a feeling that if he could, he would have had all of us vanish. It was not that he was unhappy, he was happy, but he did not want to interact with us or the other children. The children tried to interact with him but he was not willing to share himself with them, or us. He sat by himself in cold disapproval. His attitude made you feel unwelcome there as if he posed a hidden danger."

3. TROUBLING SIGNS

Archie LeBaron lives next door to the Smith family. He is a retired glassblower who worked at the Corning Glass Works fifteen miles from Savona. He lives alone, surrounded by his two dogs and three cats, one of which is a friendly vociferous Siamese cat named Sammy.

While living next door to the Smith family Archie frequently sees young Eric on his bicycle aimlessly cycling around the neighborhood for hours on end, often alone.

For reasons known only to Eric, one day in 1989 at the age of nine, he entices Sammy over to his yard, places a metal clamp around the animal's neck,— similar to those used to hold a car's radiator hose in place—and tightens it until the cat dies of asphyxiation.

LeBaron recalls seeing Eric sitting on his back steps with the cat on his lap. He notices the clamp on his lifeless cat and shouts, "What the hell are you doing?" LeBaron remembers Ted Smith coming out of the house to investigate the commotion.

"His father came out of the house and didn't say one word to him," recalls LeBaron. "He just grabbed and kicked that little boy; he must have rose three feet off the ground. I held my breath and thought,

Oh, my God, he's broken his spine. It made me sick. Ted kicked that Eric like I had never seen anybody kick anybody before."

About the cat he says, "I was so damn mad and excited. A child doesn't get himself into the frame of mind of killing a cat that way unless he's spent a lot of time thinking about it. It took me a long time to forgive him. I can't explain to you the right words, but you know you can't hate a child."

Once the anger subsides a few days later, Archie LeBaron accepts Eric's apology and agrees he can do yard work for him as a form of compensation.

Unfortunately, LeBaron does not refer the incident to any authorities, including any animal anti-cruelty organizations. Had he done so, Eric would probably have received counseling and flagged as a disturbed child who needed monitoring. Instead, he continues his existence living under the radar.

On May 7, 1993, his teacher asks him to write a creative essay, imagining something he makes out of clay suddenly comes to life. Eric Smith writes a bizarre school essay replete with symbols of evil, mutilation, and death. The boy's essay tells of a person named 'Crucified Chris, the Evil One,' making a clay figure that springs up and starts to laugh.

'I moved back,' Smith writes. 'He opened his eyes and asked me if I wanted to play the game of war. I

said, *Why not? All of a sudden, he gave me a sword and a shield. I took the first swing. I missed. He hit me with a spike in the leg... My cut was 3 inches deep.*

'I took the second swing and chopped his arm and half of his whole body. The next swing I killed him. I chopped his head off.'

The essay ends with, *'You're...ahhhh... see you in hell, my soon-to-be-dead friend.'*

The tale is disturbing, especially how it quickly becomes an essay about dying, evil, death, and mutilation. Is this Eric Smith's way of reaching out for help? Is he trying to explain the internal turmoil he feels? Is he using the essay to seek the help he needs to deal with the bullies, but does not get? Or is it the product of a deeply disturbed mind reveling in the act of killing and a forewarning of things to come?

A year before killing Derrick, Eric punches Ted Smith on the jaw while in a rage.

A few months later he physically attacks his sister, screaming, "I'm going to hurt you." He tells her he will hurt her so bad that she "will never get back up." After this incident, Eric tells his stepfather, "Dad, I need help."

Ted tells him as a youngster he would often go out to the barn and pummel a bag until he was exhausted and had spent his rage. He suggests Eric do something similar. With that, Eric leaves the room. Moments later, he returns. Ted Smith notices Eric's knuckles of both hands are ragged and bleeding. He tells his stepfather he punched a tree outside after which he appears calm.

About the same time, Marlene Heskell suggests Tammy take Eric to the same counselor her fifteen-year-old son Jason is seeing for his behavioral problems. "But she didn't seem to want to think about doing something like that," recalls Mrs. Heskell.

Jason and Eric are friends. Jason is first drawn to Eric when he sees him getting a telling-off from the school bus driver. Jason is dyslexic and also bullied at school and so sympathizes with Eric.

The week before the murder, the Smiths go camping at Babcock Hollow in the hills of Steuben County. For seven days Eric swims in the campground pool, plays video games, and chases girls. Nothing looks to be out of the ordinary and the Smiths return home Sunday, August 1.

As the weekend draws to a close, Eric Smith is looking forward to rejoining the summer camp at Conser Memorial Park the following morning.

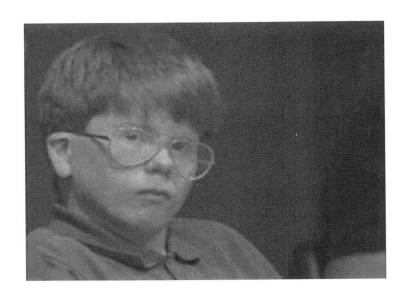

Eric Smith at Trial

4. DERRICK JOSEPH ROBIE

The Robie family has lived in Steuben County for generations. The name is a prominent one and has been since the 1800s. Dale Robie, born in Savona, marries Doreen who grew up in Towanda. Before living in Savona they live briefly in Hammondsport and Kanona. By 1993, they have been married seven years.

For the last three years they have rented a small stone house on the corner of Church and McCoy Street, on the east side of Savona. It is a prior vicarage attached to the Church of the Good Shepherd and conveniently placed a couple of blocks from the village center. Dale and Doreen live here with their two boys. Derrick is four and Dalton is eighteen months old.

Doreen has been a stay-at-home mom for the last two years but is thinking about going back to work. Dale is a typesetter who holds a steady job in Corning.

'DJ', as Derrick is fondly called, embraces life. He is a mischievous, fearless, energetic lad who has a penchant for practical jokes.

As they live so close to the church, Derrick, on one occasion, rushes out with a rubber snake he owns and places it on the sidewalk. Back in the safety of his home, with his nose pressed up against the window, he takes great delight in watching the reactions of those walking deep in thought, or in conversation on their way to Sunday service, when suddenly they see the snake in their path.

By the summer of '93, Derrick Robie has learned to ride his bicycle without training wheels, swim, tie up the dog to the back porch, and cast a fishing rod. Not only does he love fishing, he is also mad about tee-ball.

He cares deeply for animals and has a fascination with earthworms. After a night of rain, he is out the door first thing in the morning at dawn looking for worms. Finding four, which he names Mommy, Daddy, Brother, and Baby, he holds them up one at a time and gives each a kiss.

Everything he can partake in he is there, from swatting tee-balls to mixing the meatloaf, helping his father unscrew lug nuts from a car wheel, hoarding hickory nuts in his coat pocket, or pretending he is helping his father mow the lawn with his toy lawnmower. He is curious, confident, always on the go.

Derrick is a loving little boy who adores his younger brother, Dalton. They play a lot together and Derrick reads the same story to him every bedtime: Dr. Seuss's, *Green Eggs and Ham*.

The village folk who know 'DJ', cannot help but

like the sweet little boy with the blond hair, blue eyes, and a cheeky grin. People describe him as ebullient, precocious, 'a ripper of a kid'.

One of the last pictures taken of Derrick Robie

5. A CHANCE ENCOUNTER

On the same Sunday evening before summer camp, little Derrick Robie spends time at his grandparents' home on Robie Road, named for one of the earliest settlers in Savona.

They eat supper and Derrick talks excitedly about going to the recreation center the next morning, says his grandfather Henry 'Bud' Robie.

The little boy cleans his dinner plate, and he eats vanilla ice cream—which Derrick calls 'white ice cream'— for dessert.

"He was extra good that night," says Henry. "He was just all-round a good boy."

***

On August 2, 1993, Savona's residents wake to an overcast Monday morning with news they should expect inclement weather. If it rains, the authorities will have to call off the summer camp for the day. However, for a time the rain holds off, and more than sixty children from the village make their way down McCoy Street to enjoy the daily activities.

For the last three weeks, Derrick Robie, four years and ten months old, has also been going to the recreational park summer camp daily, and he loves the interaction and the events.

Usually, Doreen walks the block with her son going from their house on the corner, past the fifteen houses lining the road, to the end of the cul-de-sac where the school is on one side and Conser Memorial Park opposite, where the camp is taking place. Or on some occasions, she stands on the corner with eighteen-month-old Dalton and watches as a confident young Derrick walks toward the park lying at the end, a distance no more than 400 yards from start to finish.

Conser Memorial Park is a place Dale Robie, Derrick's father, knows well. It is where he hit his only home run. The park is named after Craig Conser, the young Savona boy who suffocated playing in a snow fort that collapsed on him when Dale himself was a young boy.

This particular morning, Dalton Robie has sore gums and is fractious. Derrick is anxious to go as it is getting on for 9:10 a.m. and they are running late. He insists he wants to leave. He stamps his feet and pleads with his mother to let him go down by himself.

Doreen says later, "I figured after three weeks he knew the path."

Right before he leaves, she folds a paper napkin and tucks it into a lunch bag. Alongside it she packs a bologna sandwich, a banana, a bottle of red Kool-Aid and some homemade peanut butter cookies.

"Derrick says, 'It's OK Mom. I'll go by myself.'

He gives his mother a kiss and says, 'I love you,' she replies, 'I love you too.' With that, he hops off the back step and is gone.

It is the first time Doreen has allowed her willful little boy his independence. It will be the last time she will see him alive.

***

Back at the recreation park a drama is unfolding.

Thirteen-year-old Eric Smith arrives at the recreation field promptly at 9 a.m. on his BMX bike. Erica Ellison, seventeen, is in charge that morning of supervising the children. However, Eric breaks the rules.

Sometime between 9 and 9:15 a.m., Ellison scolds Eric for riding his bike across a cement pavilion off-limits to the children. Ellison never tells Eric to leave the area, but the teen is angry and leaves the park, anyway. He pedals furiously away, heading up McCoy Street.

Three houses out from the park, in front of Mary Davidson's house, he sees a young boy walking along the sidewalk clutching his canvas bag containing his lunch. It is Derrick Robie.

Smith circles passed him, then doubles back, waiting for stragglers to pass who are late going into the park. When the street is empty he circles back again, calling out, "Hey, kid!" which prompts Derrick to turn around. As soon as Eric sees the young boy, he says he knew immediately he wanted to take him some place and hurt him. He finally stops his bicycle and speaks to him, a boy he knows by sight, but has never met.

Eric asks him where he is going and persuades him to take a shortcut to the summer camp through pine woods next to Mary Davidson's property.

Doreen Robie had warned her child not to talk to strangers, and so when Eric asks Derrick to come and see the shortcut he replies, "I'm not supposed to."

After several attempts at persuasion, telling the young boy by taking the shortcut he could "beat everyone else to the program," and reassuring him with, "It's okay, I'm right here," Derrick finally agrees. Eric gets off his bike and leads the boy into the woods eighty yards off the road.

***

At 9:20 a.m., Mary Davidson is getting dressed to go to work. Suddenly, Davidson's puppy, a year-old mixed-breed collie starts barking in a way she has never barked before.

"She was barking viciously in the direction of the

back lot."

***

Eric puts down his bike and allows the little boy to go ahead of him. Within minutes, he reaches around Derrick's neck and chokes him with his right arm. Derrick's will to live is strong. He drops his lunch bag, kicks his little legs, and swings his fists at the older boy in an attempt to get away. Eric Smith releases his hold on Derrick to readjust his grip and chokes Derrick with his hands. However, Derrick begins to "gasp some air" which causes Eric Smith to squeeze harder.

After about thirty seconds, Derrick no longer makes any further sounds, so Eric "figured he was dead", and places him on the grass. Derrick again begins "gasping for air". Eric empties Derrick's lunch onto the ground. He picks up the paper napkin and jams it into his mouth. He hastily pulls his fingers away as Derrick regains consciousness and bites down on Eric's finger.

***

Mary Davidson hears a scream but thinks it is a cat. "It was just one cry," she later recalls, wiping the tears from her eyes. She walks out to the back of her garden and sees nothing suspicious. Her two cats are sitting in the yard looking alert. Her dog remains at attention, too.

She dismisses the distraction and goes back into the house to prepare to leave.

***

Eric reaches for a small rock lying close by and kneeling over Derrick, strikes him three times on the right side of the head. He picks up a larger rock, this one weighing twenty-six pounds and with both hands drops it twice from a height onto Derrick's chest, and once to his midsection. At that point, Eric stops to take a drink from Derrick's drink bottle. He pours the rest of the red Kool-Aid over the young boy's face and into his bleeding wounds. He removes Derrick's pants, takes a small stick, turns Derrick over, and pushes the stick into his victim's rectum.

Eric turns Derrick over again, drags him several feet away to a less visible area and places him next to a rock pile under the canopy of some trees. He wipes the blood off his hands, and leaves the area, as he had come, on his bike.

About five minutes later, he returns to the scene to check on the body. He wants to "double, triple check to make sure" Derrick is dead. "I was worried if he wasn't there he might say something. However,

I figured if he's dead, and I believe he was, I won't have to worry about anything."

From the time he stops his bicycle to talk to Derrick to the killing, no more than ten minutes has passed. However, during that time, he inflicts horrific injuries in a frenzied killing of a complete stranger. Timings indicate although the killing lasted ten minutes, Eric Smith was with the body for nearly an hour.

***

Mary Davidson pulls out of her driveway at 10:10 a.m. She recalls seeing Eric Smith riding his bicycle in front of her house.

"He was circling around," she says. "It seemed to me like he was showing off for a girl who was walking nearby."

Eric goes back to the recreation area several times over the hour, unaffected, as if nothing has happened. Noticing the small bloodstains on his clothing, he makes certain these items go into the laundry at home on the same day.

****

Doreen Robie, the young boy's mother later recalls shortly after DJ leaves a feeling of panic sweeps over her and she senses later it is at that moment Derrick is killed.

"I swear that was the moment he died. I think he was letting us know."

"Derrick was very close to us," adds his father, Dale. "If there was any way he could have told us he was leaving, he would have tried."

However, at the time, the feeling is inexplicable, and she spends her morning looking after Dalton, still fussy with his sore gums. About 45 minutes after Derrick leaves, the expected rainstorm eventually erupts and ends the camp prematurely for the day.

Like the other parents, she rushes down McCoy Street in her car and arrives at the park to collect her son. As the other cars are loaded up with drenched children and depart, she scans the empty field looking for Derrick.

She comes across the camp supervisor. "Where's Derrick?" she asks Erica Ellison.

The young girl makes a slightly puzzled expression before telling the mother, "He didn't come today."

"Oh, my God!" is Doreen's reply. Her heart thumps in the upper-regions of her throat and overwhelming waves of panic consume her. Trying to stay calm, she contacts Dale at the printing business where he works and they notify the police at about 11 a.m.

Within the hour, kids on bicycles are scouring the neighborhood, volunteer firefighters are on the streets with a bullhorn shouting Derrick's name, and people are going door-to-door searching for him. People are scouring stores and streets looking for the missing child, including Ted and Eric Smith.

More than three hours after leaving for work, Mary Davidson comes home between sales calls. She finds the place in an uproar with police helicopters circling overhead.

"I could tell by their faces, when I pulled into McCoy Street something was terribly wrong. I never thought they would find him dead," she added. "I just didn't. That doesn't happen around here."

By 3 p.m., state troopers are pouring in by the dozen.

At 3:45 p.m., a woman's scream cuts through the air.

A local couple has found Derrick's forty-pound, forty-five-inch body at the rear of a lot covered in clover and dandelions, under a canopy of ash and hawthorn trees where children often built forts. All hope of finding him alive is gone. His lifeless broken body lies on the mossy ground, mere yards from the home he left that morning.

Even hardened investigating officers find it difficult to process what they find. One investigator says it appears the body has been staged. Besides the injuries and the post-mortem acts upon the child, his left shoe was removed and placed near his right hand, his right shoe placed near his left.

Although the canvas lunch bag had contained a banana, cookies, a sandwich and a drink, investigators find no cookies or sandwiches at the crime scene. The banana is not missing. It is squashed and is left lying in the grass.

Derrick Robie sustained severe head injuries, including multiple skull fractures and cerebral swelling, contusions, extensive tearing and bleeding of tissues in the chest, a perforation of the intestinal wall, petechial (pinpoint) hemorrhaging on the neck, face and eyes, indicating strangulation. According to the autopsy report carried out later, Derrick died from blunt trauma to the head with contributing asphyxia.

Despite the desecration of the body, no semen is found at the crime scene, or any other sexual trauma other than the stick inserted in the rectum.

***

As men and women come back from their jobs in nearby Corning and beyond, State Police close off the area. They stop, search, and question everyone entering or leaving the village.

Unaware of the unfolding tragic events of the

day dozens of volunteers meet the returning workers with muddied clothes, ashen faces, and many with tears in their eyes. They had gone out in search of the 'ripper of a lad' hoping for a positive ending. Everyone finds it difficult to accept what has taken place in their small, safe community. How is it possible one of their own has been slain with such brutality? The community is in shock, fearful, and in mourning.

Cynthia Hagadone, who lives in a trailer behind the Smith home, remembers a conversation with Eric minutes after a neighbor knocks on her door with the news the Robie boy is dead. Eric knocks on her door seconds later.

"He asked me if I had heard what happened," Hagadone recalls. We are talking about why someone would ever want to do that to a baby. He just has a blank stare—like he doesn't know either."

The Robie family is inconsolable upon hearing the news. It is tough for them, for suddenly news reporters and television crews invade the village during the same evening wanting to interview the parents of the dead boy. Most of the residents who are clustered around near the scene of the murder decline interviews when approached. However, Eric tries to get on camera. He says, "I'll do it," recalls Rose Wray, a local resident who is standing in front of Eric, Ted and Tammy Smith that evening.

Ironically, Ted Smith admonishes Eric and says, "No, you don't know anything about this."

While relatives, neighbors, and friends try to help the Robies in any way they can. Doreen replays the day's events in her mind. Why had this happened? How is it possible their beautiful boy, whom they loved so much, has been so cruelly taken from them? It is not until Tuesday the couple finally gets medically induced sleep. In the middle of the night Doreen says, "Dale jumps out of bed and says Derrick came to him in his sleep. He tells him he is okay, he never felt a thing." They take comfort from this and sleep comes a little easier after that.

The kindness shown to them by the community continues. Each day delivery people pile up flowers outside the Robies' home. They are brought to the stone-clad house where Derrick's toy lawn mower remains abandoned in the driveway.

Ministers console the parents of the boy and arrange for his funeral. Friends and neighbors continue to come by with home-baked cakes and food, while others make plans for a Labor Day country-and-western concert to help pay the costs of saying farewell to Derrick.

Not everyone is kind to the grieving parents. Many point fingers at Doreen, suggesting it is she who is responsible for the death of her son. She is an unfit mother allowing a child of that age to walk to the camp on his own. What was she thinking? They write hate mail and make abusive phone calls.

One of the many letters she receives is this one, "Maybe God will forgive you for allowing Derrick to walk the block."

She defends her actions by saying, "People don't know the circumstances, and they don't know the kind of parents we were."

Derrick died two months to the day before his fifth birthday. Doreen would have made cake and cookies and held a party for her son. Instead, on his special day she takes a big bag of homemade gingerbread cookies down to the kindergarten class he would have attended.

"They had a big party for him and sung happy birthday. That's probably been the hardest thing I've had to do since he died, next to burying him."

Almost a year later, police allow the parents access to the crime scene photos of the tiny corpse lying broken and disfigured in the brush, that was once their lively son.

Doreen says, "We only looked at one picture. It was enough."

6. WHO IS OUT THERE?

A state police criminal profiler is called to the scene. He quickly pronounces the killer as an older pedophile, possibly a sex crime parolee. While some police comb parole records looking for suspects, others search for a green pickup residents noticed parked up on McCoy Street that did not belong there.

Unaware of who has murdered the young child, it is little wonder the small community is becoming concerned for the safety of their own. Four days pass and still no one is apprehended or arrested for the murder. People are filled with fear and anguish, especially those with children.

More than a hundred residents meet on the Thursday night at the Savona Fire Department to discuss their fears. Doreen and Dale Robie are also there. Doreen addresses the crowd to answer the criticism leveled against her as a parent, for being an unfit mother in allowing her little boy to walk on his own that past Monday.

"This was just a little bit of independence I gave my son before he went to school. I didn't think four hundred yards down a sidewalk without crossing a street would be a problem. Please, if you see me, come and talk to me. I need friends now."

Savona Mayor, Michael Sweet, who lives not far from the Smith family, announces the recreation program, suspended since Derrick's death on Monday, will be reopening. Residents are split over the decision and are not convinced it is wise to resume the program, especially when the killer is still out there.

"What's happened is too traumatic," says Mary O'Connor. "Most parents won't let their children go back. They are too frightened until someone is apprehended." O'Connor questions whether there will even be sufficient supervision at the village-sponsored program.

"There's adequate supervision as there has been all summer," retorts Gary Brockway, a village trustee.

Michael Sweet says there will be no additional security at the recreation program. "We do not have staff to supervise anyone on the way to the program. We are not responsible for them on the way."

Several other residents are interested in reviving the neighborhood watch program and learning more about crime prevention. Sweet says he will arrange a meeting for them with the state police. Those who ask about increased protection for the village are told by Sweet he has already investigated assigning a sheriff's deputy to Savona.

The Robies have confidence in the investigators looking for their son's killer.

"We have a new respect for troopers," Doreen says. "They have promised us they will get this person. This happened so quickly the person who did it had to screw up in some way."

Melissa Aungst of Maple Street says the slaying has shattered the sense of security she felt growing up in Savona.

"It scares me knowing that someone's still out there, that something like this could happen in Savona. I used to walk in those fields back there (where Derrick's body was found) when I was a kid. We didn't think we had anything to worry about."

People are locking their doors for the first time and keeping their children off the streets.

"There aren't too many kids on the street and what kids there are, are in groups," says Pam Hall. "A lot of kids used to run around by themselves before this happened. Not anymore."

Pam Hall is the mother of two daughters, who resides on the same street as the Smith family on Lomoka Avenue, and oblivious to how close to the killer they are living.

7. THE INVESTIGATION

State troopers set up a command post in the village hall so they can interview every man, woman and child. Investigators interview all 68 kids signed in for the summer camp twice, including Eric Smith.

Troopers work around-the-clock searching for answers. They comb the site with metal detectors and laser equipment hoping for a clue, no matter how small. Due to the nature of the crime, they consult with psychologists hoping to determine what type of person they should be looking for. The more they search, the quicker they conclude the only person who could have committed the crime is a resident.

After interviewing over 500 people, Eric Smith is one of the first children officials question as his own mother puts him in the area at the time of the murder.

Tammy Smith, like everyone else, is horrified by what she hears and reads about the crime, and is concerned about the perpetrator who many swiftly label "an animal". She is particularly worried because thirteen-year-old Eric was near the recreation program around the time Derrick Robie was killed. After Tammy Smith asks Eric about his movements that day, she comes away with the feeling he saw something, or was threatened by something that morning.

It is after this interview Marlene Heskell notices an immediate change in Eric's demeanor. On the Wednesday he is sullen and withdrawn. If people enter a room he is in, he gets up and leaves.

Three days after the slaying Tammy takes Eric to the police command post. He enters the interview room on Thursday morning, August 5, with his mother. On this day he appears more relaxed, upbeat, and eager to help with investigations.

At about 5 p.m. that afternoon, investigators go to the Smith house and interview Eric again with the permission of his parents. They are there to clarify some minor discrepancies between his statements and those of other witnesses.

It is a casual talk around a picnic table in the Smith's yard lasting about forty-five to fifty minutes. During this time Eric reveals for the first time that he saw Derrick Robie.

Eric says he rode his bike up McCoy Street from the recreation grounds at about 9:15 a.m. He goes on to tell Investigating Officer John Hibsch he was not wearing his glasses at the time as they were broken. However, when he reached Orchard, the young boy came into view and he was walking on the opposite side of the street, near the murder scene. Smith's account of seeing Derrick Robie, however, puts Derrick some fifty to seventy-five yards away from the area where other witnesses say they saw him.

Eric then says, "Right across the street from the open field. And that's when I saw Derrick."

Officer John Hibsch recalls when Eric said that, he almost fell off his chair. "He's putting himself right on top of the crime scene. I mean, you've just got to walk across an open field and you're at the scene where the murder was."

When Hibsch asks Eric what Derrick was wearing, he is able to describe Derrick's clothing and lunch bag in detail.

Eric says, "It was kind of cool, really."

Soon after this, Eric says he needs to fetch his jacket because he is cold. He meets his mother Tammy while putting it on, and she can see he is visibly shaken. She asks him if he is okay and he says, "They asked me what it felt like when Derrick fell. They think I did it."

Eric returns, but starts getting emotional when they try to ascertain exactly where he had been standing when he last saw Derrick Robie.

"His voice breaks. He put his head down," says Hibsch. "He brings his fists up and his fists were vibrating a little bit and he goes, 'You think I killed him, don't you?'" The officers assure him they do not. However, it is one more thing that raises red flags.

When police ask Eric if he saw anything else he replies, "I'm not the type of person who would kill, hurt, or sexually molest anyone." At this stage, no one in the community has been told the nature of the crimes, especially the victim being sodomized with a stick.

The interview ends when the boy's great-grandfather Carl Peters, a retired Sheriff's deputy arrives and asks investigators to leave.

***

Approximately an hour later, at 7 p.m., state police investigators, accompanied by District Attorney John Tunney, return to Eric Smith's home to ask if they can resume the interview.

The officers reassure Eric's great-grandfather, who has assumed the role of Eric's protector, that they are not accusing Eric, but merely trying to acquire accurate details from him, since he was the last known person to see Derrick alive.

Marlene Heskell is at the Smith family home at the time and she and Carl Peters pick up on inconsistencies with Eric's account of events.

Marlene also notices while Eric's account is clear up to the point when he saw Derrick Robie, he falters as he tries to describe where he went and what he did after he passes the intersection.

***

Neighbors watch that same Thursday evening as Carl Peters stands by while investigators videotape his great-grandson Eric riding his bike from the end of McCoy Street to the Davidson's house. Eric rides back and forth several times, at different speeds, and is timed with a stopwatch.

Steuben County District Attorney John Tunney will not explain why this is being done. He confirms Eric has agreed to have his actions videotaped. State police Inspector Charles Wood says young Eric Smith, "appeared to be enjoying the attention" from police, who were worried he was making up stories.

Investigating Officer John Hibsch is suspicious. Eric is unable to explain why he can describe in detail Derrick's clothing and lunch bag the preschooler carried that day from across the street without wearing his glasses. He had broken those mere days before, but now he is having trouble describing what a police officer is holding in his hand as the officer walks the same path Derrick walked during the re-enactment.

Again, during the reenactment, Eric points out where he had seen Derrick, but can make out only the outline of an investigator playing the role of

Derrick.

Marlene was surprised at the level of detail Eric was able to give without the aid of his glasses. "He can't see more than twenty feet in front of him without them," she says.

Because it is getting dark, the parties agree to return the next day to reenact the scene.

To check his story officers take him to the area the following day and ask him to ride his bike to the spot where he saw Derrick.

Again, there are problems with Eric's account. The officers begin to question whether Eric even encountered Derrick that day. They need to know for sure before wasting time pursuing a false lead. Investigators subsequently interview Eric for two hours at the command post in the presence of his great-grandfather, Carl Peters.

However, when he contradicts himself during the interviews with police and offers up details no one else should know, he falls under suspicion, but still they do not consider him a suspect.

Ted Smith is also present and asks for a break during the investigation, which the officers grant. The interview resumes and Ted Smith, unwittingly, gives Eric some red Kool-Aid.

On seeing the drink he becomes enraged. He takes one swipe at it and knocks it to the ground. The investigators note his behavior with interest.

His family, unaware of the connection, is bewildered by his outburst. Even at this point police still did not consider Eric a suspect. Rather, officers feel Eric has witnessed something extremely traumatic, perhaps the murder itself, and there is now a block. They are finding difficulty in getting through to him.

During the interview, Eric is evasive about whether he had seen Derrick. At the end of the interview, police still are not sure he had.

They tell Carl Peters they feel Eric did not see anything. Eric is told this and Marlene Heskell notices Eric's spirits rise.

***

After the interview ends, investigators do not contact the Smith family the next day, August 7. This is Saturday, the day of Derrick Robie's funeral.

Meanwhile, forty State Police investigators working in teams pursue different investigative angles. They talk to parolees. They interrogate the owner of the green truck parked on McCoy Street and unfamiliar to villagers. They comb registers at area motels for names of people who were passing through on the day. They are frustrated, for despite interviewing over 500 people they are no closer to solving the crime.

Eric's own family is wondering about the inconsistencies of his story. His grandfather Red Wilson admits, "There was a discrepancy in his story. In no way did we feel he had done it. We felt he knew something. Maybe somebody had threatened him. That's why he wouldn't tell."

Even Ted Smith felt there was a problem. He later says, "Something inside me kept saying, 'There's something wrong here. Something's not right.'"

Close friends, John and Marlene Heskell thought the same thing.

Eric spends almost every night after the murder at their home. The night after the killing, August 2, Ted, Tammy, Eric and Holly Smith visit Marlene and John Heskell and stay past midnight. The night is consumed by discussions of the murder. Both families agree the killer has to be an outsider. Ted Smith suggests when the killer is caught he is "hung on Main Street". While the conversation takes place, young Eric sits at the table watching, but says nothing.

Marlene says during the week of Derrick's slaying, Eric visits them every day and spends three nights at their home, including the evening of the 2nd. The following morning Jason Heskell sits at the breakfast table with Eric and together they play a detective game of sorts, trying to guess who killed Derrick Robie.

During that week his behavior for the most part, is normal, remembers Marlene. He plays Nintendo, listens to country music, and rides his bike. However, there are little things she notices as odd. He is afraid to be near windows at night and repeatedly asks about the punishment one could expect if the murderer turns out to be a kid.

While he is with them he marks a map of the neighborhood published in the *Corning Leader* newspaper. The map shows the Robie residence on Church Street near the intersection of McCoy Street, and the area near the recreation field where Derrick was walking the morning he disappears. His body is found in woods at the back of a vacant lot on McCoy.

Jason says he worked from a copy traced on a notebook paper. He draws a triangle shape around the woods, showing several possible entrances to the area the killer could have taken. While he draws, Eric watches and eats his cereal.

After Jason puts his pen down, he says he watches as Eric draws a line from the Robie home, down McCoy Street and off into the woods. It indicates to Marlene Eric has some knowledge of the crime,

There is also a side to Eric that Marlene discovers later that surprises her. She learns that Eric and Jason had an argument and as they pass the church

Eric shouts, "The devil rules!" A phrase that Jason says later is written on the rubber edge of Eric's sneakers. Jason goes on to tell his mother Eric had walked onto Route 266 and deliberately stood in the path of oncoming vehicles, assuring him, "They'll move. They always do."

She goes back to the conversation where Eric had turned to her and asked what would happen if it turned out the killer was a child. She remembers replying, "I seriously think they would need psychiatric help."

His response was nonchalant. "Oh, okay."

During this time, Marlene is at home with good friend Nancy Steiniger, a Steuben County Corrections Officer. Eric, knowing Nancy's occupation asks her about DNA. He wants to know what it is and what it shows. While Marlene and Nancy discuss the Robie case out on the porch, Eric is told to go inside. Instead he remains perched in a window, listening and watching.

***

While Eric is staying with Marlene, she cannot help but notice his fascination with death and violence, not only in his choice of reading matter, but his morbid fascination with, and comments on newspaper obituaries. While police are searching for the killer, he is reading about the crime in her newspapers and underlining certain sections.

As details of the case start to leak out, Nancy Steiniger mentions to her friend the consensus is that a child committed the murder. The assumption centers on the fruit left at the crime. An adult might have discarded the banana, but a child, perhaps one who does not like bananas, would have deliberately squashed it.

Marlene starts doing her own investigation. She goes off to the store and buys ingredients for banana sundaes. When she returns, she asks the kids in the house, including Eric who is there, who wants a banana sundae. Eric only wants ice cream, nuts, and syrup. When she questions this, saying, "I thought all kids like bananas."

His reply is, "No, I don't like bananas."

Afterwards, Marlene jokingly phones her friend Nancy and says, "Eric doesn't like bananas and I'm scared."

***

Early Saturday morning Eric experiences the Heskells' wrath and disappointment.

Eric Smith was again staying the night. Shortly after 2:30 a.m. Jason awoke to heat on his face. He discovers Eric is holding a burning cigarette to the end of his nose. When Jason questions his behavior, Eric replies that he was just trying to see how close he could get. In addition, he says he wanted to wake

Jason up as he was scared.

The burn is so bad that Jason's skin blisters and Eric, after apologizing profusely, fetches ice and cold steaks to reduce the damage.

Marlene cannot help but notice her son's face in the morning and when she discovers what has transpired, she is furious. She is thoroughly upset and disgusted by Eric's behavior. So much so, she tells him he will no longer be welcome to stay over in the future.

As she drives Eric home that Saturday morning she sees him rummaging through her ashtray. She asks him what he is doing, and he tells her he wants to have a cigarette before he goes home.

Marlene tells him to stop it as she does not want him to smoke in front of her. Eric glares at her, lights a cigarette butt and defiantly smokes as she drives. She is so flustered she speeds through a red light on her way to the Smith home. Eric opens the door on arrival, gets out, and abruptly says goodbye.

It is also on Saturday John Heskell goes to the State Police command post in Savona and turns in the map on which Eric had drawn a line to the site of Derrick's death.

John tells the police he is turning in the map because Eric had bragged to him that the authorities did not think he had witnessed the killing. Heskell suspects he had.

***

On Sunday, John Heskell goes fishing with his son Jason, Ted Smith, and Eric at Keuka Lake. Heskell and Ted Smith fish offshore from a boat. John notices Ted Smith is watching Eric constantly, but says nothing of his concerns to John.

That evening, Ted and Tammy Smith excuse themselves from prior dinner plans at the Heskells' home. Ted tells them his sinuses are plaguing him. However, it is a poor excuse. Eric's immediate family has also started to dig a little deeper to see what Eric knows and the more they do, the less confident they are that he was just a bystander.

As police scramble to build a case, Eric's great-grandfather makes his own observations. Carl Peters calls a family meeting, and with the rest of his family members, sits down and questions Eric. His grandfather, Red Wilson, is among those pressing the teenager to tell the family what he knows.

Tammy Smith says, "We stressed how important it was that he tell the truth, that this was serious. And if someone had threatened him, to tell us. If he knew anything, to tell us."

After half an hour of prodding to reveal the truth by various family members, Eric unexpectedly turns to his mother, stepfather, grandfather, and great-grandfather and confesses, "Mom, I did it. I snapped, and I done it. I'm sorry, Mom. I'm sorry. I killed that little boy."

Carl Peters reveals, after that, "All hell broke loose." Tammy Smith loses control on hearing his shocking confession, and shaking her son violently, demands more details. She screams at him and demands to know why he had done it. His response is, "I don't know. I don't know. I don't know why. I'm sorry. I'm sorry." All the time Tammy Smith is "yelling and screaming and bawling and everything at once".

Eric bursts into tears.

Tammy is no stranger to grief. Her two younger brothers died in a drowning accident many years ago, but this news is too much for her to bear. She reacts particularly badly to this revelation, and at that point, the family is more concerned for Tammy's well-being, than Eric's. Carl Smith says, "She's an epileptic. I thought we were going to lose her."

After the mayhem subsides, Carl Peters picks up the phone and calls Sgt. Ronald Bates asking for a meeting with District Attorney, John Tunney. He tells Bates, Eric is the killer and "the boy needs help."

"It was probably one of the toughest things he's done in his life," says Karl Secondo, county undersheriff, and Carl Peters' former partner.

Carl Peters takes this route to handle the matter 'as peaceful and as quiet as we can'. He specifically asks to avoid the involvement of the state police, the prospect of a public arrest, and the possibility of a Grand Jury proceeding, or other preliminaries. At no time does he think his great-grandson will be tried in a criminal court, despite the crime, due to his young age.

D.A. Tunney persuades Carl Peters that Captain Walter DeLap, from the Bureau of Criminal Investigation has to be notified to take Eric's statement. Finally, Peters agrees for DeLap to come to the office. In turn, Carl contacts his family and asks them to bring Eric.

Two days after their second interrogation of Eric Smith, and six days after Derrick's death, Eric Smith arrives at the Steuben Country Office Building on the evening of August 8 to make a full confession. With him is his mother, stepfather, and grandfather, Red Wilson.

The District Attorney leaves the room before the interview begins because, as he explains to Carl Peters, he will have to prosecute the case and does not want to witness the statement. He makes no promises that Eric will not be prosecuted criminally. He agrees Eric needs help and suggests psychiatric evaluations should start within the next few days.

Before the interview starts, DeLap reads Eric his *Miranda* rights carefully, rephrasing them so he can understand them in simple terms. This is something that will be contested later by Eric's attorney. DeLap asks Eric if he understands his rights, and he replies he does, except he wants to know what an attorney is. DeLap tells him an attorney is a lawyer, and this satisfies him.

Ground rules are set. Although family members can be present during the interrogation, they are not permitted to interrupt.

For the next three hours, Eric is calm and composed as investigators Captain Walter DeLap and Ronald Bates listen to what happened that fated morning. As the facts unfold, they match perfectly with the physical evidence and condition of the body. The delivery of the confession is given in a flat, matter-of-fact tone, as if he were reading a laundry list.

All the while Ted Smith sits against the wall behind the teen. Eric's great-grandfather, Carl Peters, sits behind the boy facing a wall, with his ear towards him. They are shocked by what they hear. Eric relays his recollection with remarkable detail of what he did to Derrick.

"I looked to the left and saw a little kid with blond hair, a whitish t-shirt, carrying a bluish/brown with designs, bag. He was walking towards Rec. I turned around and went up behind him and when I was within ten feet I said, 'Hey, kid!' The kid turned around as I caught up to him. At that point, I knew I wanted to take him somewhere and hurt him.

"I asked the kid if he wanted to go to Rec by way of a shortcut, through the woods and beat everybody there. The kid said, 'No, I'm not supposed to.' I said, 'It's okay, I'm right here.' The kid then followed me through the empty lot. I let the kid go in front of me.

"When we got inside the trees, I put my arm around his neck. I was standing behind him. The kid then dropped his lunch. I continued squeezing harder as the kid made fists and swung his arms trying to get away. I was going to hold him against a tree and choke him with my hands. As I started to release him, he made a noise like he was trying to gasp some air, a weird noise. So I said, 'forget it!' and squeezed harder. I let go after thirty seconds or so. He didn't make any noise so I let him down on the ground. His eyes were closed and I don't know if he was breathing. There was a little rock lying beside him and I hit him in the head three times. I then picked up a bigger rock. I threw the rock with both hands, down onto his head. At this point blood began running from his nose and the rock fell to the side. Two more times I picked up the rock and threw it onto his head. I then picked up another big rock. I threw that rock into the middle of his chest.

"Now I remember while he was lying on the ground, before I hit him with any rock, he was gasping for air. I dumped his lunch out onto the ground which consisted of a sandwich, cookie, koolaid (sic), plastic reusable container, and something else which I can't recall. Also, I saw a paper napkin and put it into his mouth. As I tried to stuff the baggie in his mouth, he bit me. It hurt but left no marks. I pulled my finger and the baggie out and threw the baggie down. I then began hitting him in the head with the rocks.

"I picked up the koolaid (sic) and poured it on his face on the right side of his temple area where I had hit him with the small rock and on his chest. At this point, I don't know whether I had pulled down his pants, or not. I must have taken them down. I then flipped him over and put the stick up his butt. I then left the area. After about five minutes at Rec I went back to the body. I was worried if he wasn't there he might say something. I figured if he's dead, and I believe he was, I won't have to worry about anything. When I arrived back at Rec it started thundering and Bill Horn, the director, told everyone to go home."

DeLap notes that at the beginning of his confession Eric has a downcast look. However, as the events unfold at one point during the interview

Smith becomes so animated DeLap has to remind Eric, "This is not some fun thing we're doing. Let's remember what we're here for. Let's calm down."

What Eric does not tell anyone in the room, is why he was angry, or why he killed Derrick. All he can say is he was so angry he wanted to hurt someone, and when he saw Derrick, vulnerable, and on his own, he knew he wanted to hurt him.

He does however admit he deliberately lured Derrick into the woods for the killing so no one would see what he was doing.

More than forty law enforcement personnel had spent 30,000 hours trying to solve the murder, interviewing almost every inhabitant in Savona. When they first started their investigation, the fact that a child could be the perpetrator, had never been thought probable. However, as the investigation progressed, Eric Smith had moved from a person of interest to the prime suspect. After his full confession, an arrest was the only conclusion.

They dreaded breaking the news to the small community the following morning.

8. NEWS OF THE ARREST

At a noon conference at the Savona village hall, state troopers make the announcement that they have made an arrest. The arrest brings to a close a week in which the small community had lashed out to the unknown outsider they branded an 'animal' for killing little Derrick Robie.

For days Savona's inhabitants had raged at the stranger who had stealthily entered their community and killed one of their babies. They had imagined all sorts of undesirables responsible, even accusing men who lived among them.

The authorities tell the residents of Savona one of their own is responsible. Thirteen-year-old Eric Smith has made a full confession.

The villagers had had faith in the 'classic older man pedophile' the criminal profiler had described. People could deal with that scenario. But a child? Never had they suspected another child, especially one of their own. People are in shock on hearing the news, but when they hear the murderer is Eric Smith, they are numb. The nondescript, nerdy teenager does not look like the killer he is. Those who know him cannot reconcile the helpful, genial, affectionate child as the monster who lives among them.

There are none more shaken than the Heskells who had opened their home to him and treated him like one of their own. Fifteen-year-old Jason is so traumatized by Eric's arrest Marlene has to seek counseling for him.

After Eric's arrest, State Police ask the Heskells for permission to search their home due to Eric's staying there in the past. They concede. Before the police arrive, John Heskell goes through his son's room. In the closet he finds a drawing that disturbs him. A few nights earlier, Marlene had ordered Eric out of the closet which Eric said he was cleaning.

The drawing Heskell finds is addressed to a girlfriend Eric often phoned when he stayed overnight. The girlfriend attends a special-education program in Bath, with his son Jason. Jason tells his father Eric and the girl would often use him to exchange notes between each other.

The picture John finds is that of a man and woman having oral sex. Scrawled across the bottom of the picture is the caption, "Fun is a crime."

After Eric is arrested, the Smiths and the Heskells continue to visit one another. One question that bothers Eric, which he needs his father to ask, is whether the Heskells hate him. They assure Ted, they don't hate Eric. Marlene goes on to say, "We hate what he did to Derrick. We're discouraged, we're disappointed, we're very, very upset with him. The question is Why? How do you hurt anyone so bad?"

***

The death of one child and the arrest of another soon cause a schism in the community. The murder, especially one of a child, swamps the community with anger. Eric is the baby-faced monster who deserves to go to jail and never come out. However, there are those consumed with guilt for Eric, the child they failed, the one they see as a victim of circumstance.

The Smith family becomes the target of relentless gossip as villagers speculate on Eric's motive and home background that would cause his heinous actions.

While the village showers one family with sympathy, the other becomes a pariah. The Smiths take down their Christmas lights adorning the house and draw down the window shades. Relatives bring bags of groceries to their closed front door. The occupants now speak to others through their attorney.

Not everyone is kind to the Robie family either after the loss of their son. The fundraising concert organized to help pay for Derrick Robbie's funeral divides the community even further. Some phone the Robies to criticize them for allowing friends to organize the event, saying Eric and his family need the money more to pay for his defense.

"I suspect it would have been easier for us if the suspect had not been a Savona resident," reflects Wayne Beardsley, the principal of Campbell-Savona Elementary School. "It just dumbfounds you."

The Smith family is at a loss to explain why their son would commit such a heinous crime. There has never been any overt sign of mental illness. Although they do admit their son has indulged in some odd behavior, besides killing Archie LeBaron's Siamese cat. They recall two years after killing the cat, a schoolmate died in a car crash. Eric phoned the family on several occasions asking to speak to the deceased boy. It was not due to Eric not understanding the youth was dead. He did. His calls seemed to provide him with perverse sadistic pleasure in causing distress to the family every time he phoned.

Suddenly, Savona is on the map. People, from near and far, travel to the village to visit the crime scene for morbid curiosity. Mary Davidson, whose field it is where Derrick Robie was killed, is forced to employ a contractor to plow up the field in a bid to stop the curiosity.

The media descend on the small settlement and interviews people who knew both families. Some people craving for fame but no fortune are happy to talk. For others, the reality of the situation is too painful and they decline the offer to air their views.

Those that talk say Eric Smith seemed to be a polite teenager who was struggling with the normal things someone of his age faces. Sarah Farnsworth, a twenty-year-old recreation program counselor, who knew Eric since he was in kindergarten says, "He was really a sweet kid. But there was something about him that just wasn't right." She quickly goes on to say, "I know Eric had a bad temper but I don't know what anyone could have done to make him that mad."

Friends and neighbors all relay similar stories. Eric was hyperactive, he had a quick and bad temper, and was quick to fight. When Eric failed fourth grade he started hanging around with younger children and gained the reputation of being a tough guy who was quick to bully those younger. In addition, he too was the victim of bullying.

Shock and disbelief cloak the village as they try to understand the events. They wonder who is at fault and suffer collective guilt over a murder that has shattered the very fabric of their community. What did they miss? What could they have done differently? Is it the fault of Eric's parents? Is it the negligence of Derrick's mother? Or is it a far greater societal issue that is to blame? What evil could drive a child to kill?

People started looking at their own children in a different light. "It makes me wonder if my kids could do this," said Janice Pettit, a friend of Eric's mother, Tammy Smith.

Barbara Campbell, the village clerk, places the blame at the door of mass media for exposing children to so much material even open-minded adults find upsetting or offensive for its sexual and violent content.

"Maybe some kids can't tell the difference between reality and fantasy," she says. "All I know is a little boy walking down the street to the park was killed and no one can explain it in any way that makes sense."

Two weeks after the killing, his biological father, Randy Hevner, also feels partially to blame. He says he had spoken to his son two weeks ago at a softball game and had seen no signs that there was anything wrong. However, he wishes he had gotten to know his son better. He says on seeing his son in handcuffs at his arraignment, "It tore me right up. I wished I could have taken him and gotten him out of there. A kid just doesn't kill another kid and not have problems. Just what those problems are, I don't know."

Becky Feehan, a retired English teacher, feels there is no point proportioning blame. "We have to face the fact there's another family in this town torn apart by the tragedy. It's an evil beyond understanding. A child isn't born to kill another child."

"There's a feeling of 'What have we done to cause this to happen?'" says the Rev. Frank Edmunds, whose Church of the Good Shepherd is next door to the Robies' home.

"It's a tragedy for two families, but it is also a tragedy for a small village," says Howard Farnsworth, a retired high school teacher who lives next to the dandelion-covered lot where Derrick's body was found.

"We're all hurting by this thing."

9. THE FUNERAL

When Dale and Doreen are finally given back their son to bury, they struggle with their grief and the outpouring from others.

More than 700 people, still in shock of what has happened, turn out to shuffle past the open casket. Michael Sweet says, "You could see in his face the pain he must have gone through."

The mood is somber on Saturday morning as some 150 mourners squeeze into the stained-glass sanctuary built to seat 100. Skies continue to darken outside as the strains of a Reba McEntire song, "If I had Only Known", can be heard coming from inside the church.

"Derrick loved Reba McEntire", says Jim Cook of Monroeton, Pennsylvania, one of the boy's grandfathers. He will deliver the eulogy at the service.

Jim Cook describes Derrick as a bundle of energy and interests. He was, "Babe Ruth, Nimrod, Izaak Walton, Huckleberry Finn, Dr. Doolittle, the Tasmanian Devil and two sticks of dynamite packed into a three-foot frame."

Derrick probably arrived in heaven in the morning, Cook continues, "Before the sun had set, he had worn out two angels, and put another one in the hospital with a bent halo and a dislocated wing."

People who knew the little boy well, cannot help but smile at the accurate portrayal. Tears spring up as people are reminded of the senselessness of it all.

The funeral service is presided over by Mr. Strong in the 145-year-old Savona Federated Church of which the Robies are regular members. Pastor Strong tells the mourners, "The real question is, where was God? The answer to that is, God was with Derrick, that his heart broke, and a part of him died when Derrick died."

As the mourners file out of the church, rain begins to fall. There is not much talking immediately after the funeral. People walk to their cars consumed by their inner thoughts, sometimes stopping to share a hug. A cloudburst drenches a smaller group of people gathering to attend the burial service at Seaman's Cemetery.

"Tears from heaven," says Martha Andersen of Savona.

But faith is often not a complete comfort when a child is lost, she goes on to say. "People want to know, 'Where was God?' How could this happen to a good Christian family?" asks Andersen, who lost her own daughter to a drunken driver in 1991.

They bury Derrick Robie in the village cemetery, off Route 415. He is dressed in his tee-ball uniform, with a bat and ball placed in the coffin at his side. As the coffin is lowered, rain continues to fall.

Later at the wake held in the basement of the church, people begin to seek comfort from one another in recalling happier memories of the small boy. Church dinners after a funeral are a tradition in small communities like Savona. "It brings people together and starts them talking," says Millie Allen, a relative of the Robie family.

As numbness and disbelief give way to more cheerful memories, those who attend the funeral service say the eulogy by Cook, beautifully captured the personality of Derrick.

"Derrick would be looking for the rainbow," muses Al Allen. "People get mad at God," he continues, "but he never promised we'd be exempt from pain. He promised he'd be there to give us strength and comfort."

When asked to describe her eldest son, Doreen says, "He was my cute little firecracker. He was full of energy, and we were very close because I was home with him. At times, he was a little comedian. He liked to tell me Reba (McEntire) was playing on television, and I'd get out there and it would be Marty Brown or someone I didn't like. And he'd run away from me and I'd try to catch him and tickle him."

Derrick was also the unofficial mayor of Savona.

"He sat on the corner on his bike and waved to cars that went by," recalls his mother, Doreen. "Everybody remembers him doing that."

"Derrick was a feisty, friendly little boy," says the Rev. Neil Strong of the Savona Federated Church. "He'd wave hello to everyone. He would go nonstop through a day."

When Dale Robie is asked about his son Derrick, he says it all in a few words, "He was all boy."

The sun has come out by the early afternoon as people begin to leave the church basement with empty casserole dishes tucked under their arms.

***

On Wednesday night, August 11, Dale Robie speaks briefly at the start of a public prayer service at Campbell-Savona Elementary School. The same school Eric attended.

"Hopefully, I'll get through this okay," he tells the gathering of about 350 people sitting on bleachers and folding chairs in the school's gymnasium. He takes the opportunity to thank the residents of Savona for the support they have shown the family.

"Since the slaying, many people have told me a story of how Derrick touched their lives. Derrick was a people person. He enjoyed his time, and he lived every moment."

As his voice breaks, he tries to ease the tension in the quiet gymnasium. "There's no time limit, is there?" the boy's father tries to joke.

***

Nearly a year passes before an inscription is erected on the previously plain grave marked by a cross. The shiny black headstone reads:

In our hearts
You will remain
Forever young

The words are taken from the lyrics of a Rod Steward song, 'Forever Young' which is a song Doreen frequently sang to her eldest son.

The polished headstone stands at the head of the grave, a likeness of Derrick etched into the stone. He's smiling, his blond hair combed neatly over his forehead, a striped pullover shirt open at the neck.

Etched above his name, Derrick Joseph Robie, is a reminder of his love of baseball; a bat, ball and glove, and a cap with the initials DJ.

Plants grow from several pots flanking the headstone including one from a figure of a white lamb lying in front of it. To one side is a feeder filled with bird seed. Also adorning the stone is a small green cement frog, a lawn ornament left there by

Dalton, Derrick's younger brother.

"Both boys like frogs," says their mother. "Dalton has one just like it here at home that we keep out in our garden."

The Robies come to the graveyard often to visit their son. Every Christmas eve, without fail, they light a battery-operated Christmas tree for the little boy who should have been there to join the family for the festive season.

***

Dale and Doreen Robie find it difficult to stay in the house on McCoy Street. There are too many memories and little Dalton moves from room to room asking for his brother, wondering where he is.

The family says, "It is now time for us to start over as our one-and-a-half-year-old son doesn't understand why his brother isn't riding next to him in the car, or eating cereal with him in the morning. We will stay in the community but not on this street. Savona now means more than just a town as we have felt every teardrop on our shoulders of mourners for our son."

Before Christmas, the family packs up their belongings and move nearly a mile out of Savona to live on family-owned land to start over. Despite the move, photographs of the happy little boy, always smiling, line the walls of their new dining room. In addition, they have kept mementoes to keep his memory alive.

Doreen Robie remembers during the move unpacking a little gold box she always kept on the coffee table and finds a hickory nut inside, placed there by small hands. "I left it there, put the top back on and put it back on the shelf."

There is a letter of condolence from the president. There is also a poem written by Mary Davidson that begins,

Remember me in early spring,
When tee-ball fields with laughter ring…

***

The village comes together before winter sets in and clears the base of the hill where Derrick was killed to create a community park in memory of one of their sons. One of the first volunteers to help clear the field is Carl Peters, the man who had to report his great-grandson to the authorities for Derrick's murder.

"I went to him and thanked him and hugged him," recalls Doreen Robie. "We hold no bad feelings for anyone in Eric Smith's family—except for Eric."

On the knoll, overlooking the two new baseball fields, a crab apple tree, and a flagpole, is a 42-inch bronze statue of Derrick. Derrick's great uncle, Steve Hughey, crafted the statue in his workshop in Corning. It is erected in the summer of '94 on the spot where he died, to honor the little resident everyone loved and mourns.

Doreen Robie says of the statue, "As horrid and as negative as this has been, you look for something to try to turn positive. I hope people can look at the statue and just remember what childhood was supposed to be about because we've lost it somewhere...with all these teenagers that have gone totally haywire. I feel kind of naïve because I thought I tried to keep him from everything."

Her words strike a chord with the community, because beneath the statue of their smiling boy, swinging a tee-ball bat is the inscription, 'A gentler reminder of what childhood is supposed to be.'

Both parents refuse to forget their eldest son. "I think Dory and I talk about him like he was in the next room most of the time," says Dale Robie. "I think if we didn't, we'd feel pretty negative."

***

The Robies considered for a while having another child and they talk about adoption, but in the end decide against both.

"I had a real hard time with that," says Dale. "I

put so much time and energy into that one that I can't do it again."

The pain has diminished since Derrick's murder, but it never really goes away.

"We still have days," Doreen Robie says. "I have a terrible time on Derrick's birthday. Christmas Eve is really tough. But if I crawl into a hole and give up, evil wins."

10. FIRST COURT APPEARANCE

On August 11, 1993, Eric Smith makes his first court appearance and waives his right to a preliminary hearing. The Bath Courthouse is packed.

The handcuffed young boy enters the courtroom at 10:00 a.m. surrounded by a posse of plain-clothed and uniformed police. The men push their way through the crowds who are there hoping to get a glimpse of the red-headed 'devil' who killed the innocent preschooler.

There are so many members of the media and press present, along with curious onlookers, many cannot fit into the room.

In the path cleaved by the police follow a few of Eric's relatives who are seated on make-shift folding chairs in the front of the over-stuffed courtroom. Dale and Doreen Robie are also present but remain at the back of the room.

The appearance of the large burly policemen is in stark contrast to the young teenager who does not even come to their shoulders and looks years younger than his age. His demeanor is solemn, bookish even, accentuated by the oversized aviator glasses, the same glasses that had been the clue to his guilt. It is hard to reconcile that such a monstrous crime has been committed by one who looks so benign.

Looking at the young boy dressed in black formal trousers and a mustard yellow polo shirt, outwardly, he appears calm. His face is deadpan, with not a flicker of an emotion. As he sits down his lawyer, Kevin P. Bradley of Canisteo introduces himself, and as he explains the procedure to his young client. In the meantime a policeman removes his handcuffs. Eric sits back in his chair and coolly waits for the arrival of Bath Town Justice Leon F. Taggart and quietly picks his nails.

Attorney Kevin Bradley is a man who cares deeply about the law and justice. His job as a defense lawyer for the state means low wages by comparison to some of his colleagues. As a husband and father of four children, his wages go to them first and he cares little for the fact his suit is a little worn and threadbare.

His adversary, prosecutor John Tunney, has the utmost respect for Bradley. He says that there is no better man to take on this case for the defense. "Sound, quality defense work is important to me as it is to the defendant. There are many capable defense attorneys in the county, but Kevin does only criminal defense. This makes Bradley one of the most experienced defense attorneys in the country. Bradley's gift is an ability to explain difficult legal points to jurors and make them appreciate the importance of their job—a task that could be especially important in the Smith case," Tunney said.

Justice Taggart takes the bench and Bradley waives Eric's right to a preliminary hearing. Eric can barely see over the top of the bench as he tells the judge he understands the procedure.

Judge Taggart orders Eric to be returned to Monroe County Children's Center in Rochester without setting bail. The entire hearing lasts less than ten minutes.

Eric holds out his arms and the policeman puts on the handcuffs. Again, officers form a wedge and lead him out of the courtroom to a holding room.

Reporters and spectators try to get a better view as he is again moved, this time out of the building. As he shuffles through the door a family member calls out, "We love you, Eric."

He looks back but says nothing and is placed in a waiting police car. As the car pulls off, he raises a hand in greeting to the photographers, both hands still manacled.

11. FEELING BETRAYED

Following Eric Smith's confession, the family feels betrayed by the justice system. Instead of pressing charges against the thirteen-year-old in Family Court, where he could be remanded to a juvenile treatment facility for the 'help' they feel he needs, the prosecutor almost immediately announces he plans to charge Eric with murder, and requires him to stand trial in an adult criminal court.

Under New York's juvenile offender's law, minors as young as thirteen may be tried as adults when charged with murder; to be tried as an adult for any other serious violent crime, a youngster must be at least fourteen-years-old. Although the statute allows the criminal court judge to transfer such a case to Family Court, the judge may not do so without the consent of the prosecutor.

Eric Smith pleads not guilty and the day after his confession, on August 9, 1993, authorities house him with some 40 juvenile offenders at the Monroe County Department of Social Services Detention Center, three miles south of Rochester. He is sent here as Steuben County has no certified State facility to hold juveniles. At Monroe he has his own room with a bed, desk, chair, toilet, and closet. He is also allowed to meet with teachers.

On August 11, 1993, he appears briefly at the

court proceeding in nearby Bath. Here he pleads not guilty to the murder of Derrick Robie. His court appearance lasts less than three minutes amid tight security and intense media coverage. During that time, Kevin Bradley tells Judge Donald Purple that defense had hired a lawyer who has deemed his client fit to stand trial.

As Judge Purple talks to the defendant, Eric Smith the boy replies in monosyllables. "Yeah" and "Uh, huh" is all that is said by the teen.

As Eric is led handcuffed and expressionless to a waiting police car, members of his family yell out, "I love you!" As the car pulls away from the sidewalk, he leans forward, hands still cuffed and attempts to wave in return.

On the return journey to the detention center he is his usual silent self, the quiet broken by only one question to the officer in the car, "So, do you think I'll be home next week?"

12. PSYCHOLOGICAL EVALUATIONS

Eric's appointed lawyers, Kevin P. Bradley, a man known as a capable lawyer and for his attention to detail, and Joseph Pelych, five years younger than Bradley and a former assistant Steuben County district attorney.

"He doesn't seem to understand how much of his time he's looking at spending in custody," Bradley says. "It's almost like he's unaffected. His concerns are like any kid's. He seems like he looks. He seems intelligent, but comes across as a child. He had some question about whether there had been newspaper articles about the case, and when his parents are coming to visit." He goes on to say during his initial visits in getting to know Eric better, "He talked about wrestling, about smoking cigarettes. My basic impression is, this is a kid and there's nothing bizarre about it."

However, Bradley and Pelych soon realize their client is a seriously disturbed youngster. Bradley pleads with the prosecutor to have the boy examined by a psychologist or psychiatrist before condemning him to an adult criminal trial and a possible life sentence.

In May 1994, the defense moves pursuant to the case from a Criminal Court to the Family Court. In support of the motion, the defense alleges the case is an exceptional one warranting removal because psychological evidence reveals the defendant's act is the result of a lifelong mental disease—a pathological rage disorder.

With the court's approval, which is required largely for financial reasons (the doctor's fees will be paid from public funds), Eric's attorney asks two mental health professionals to examine Eric. They are Dr. Peter Cormack, a Penfield N.Y. clinical psychologist, and Dr. Stephen Herman, a Yale trained Connecticut pediatrician and child psychiatrist.

McCormack's fee is $150 an hour with the initial limit for the testing at $3,000. Steven Herman's fees cost the Steuben County $6,490. He charges the county $275 an hour for his services; twenty-three-and-a-half hours in total, consisting of eight-and-a-half hours in interviews and fifteen hours in travel time.

Dr. Cormack conducts both intelligence and projective tests, and concludes, "Eric harbors a great deal of anger and rage...that relates to feelings of rejection and/or abandonment....On occasions, when this rage builds up to a sufficient intensity that it is directly expressed, he can become rather detached from his own actions, taking little personal responsibility for what is occurring and not giving consideration to anything other than what is happening in the moment....Depressed moods, as well as anger, including angry or hostile outbursts, result when his efforts at control do not serve to block painful feelings.

"Although Eric does not demonstrate any signs of significant cognitive or intellectual impairment, the mental disease from which he suffers is such that he was unable to appreciate either the legal or moral implications of his actions at the time of the crime. It is doubtful that he appreciates these factors even at the present time."

Dr. Stephen Herman sees two sources for Eric's intermittent explosive disorder: first, the medication Tammy took during her pregnancy, and second, Ted Smith's physical and mental abuse.

He orders numerous studies of Eric, including physical and neurological examinations.

His findings are as follows: "Eric was born with certain constitutional or organic vulnerabilities... born with fetal trimethadione syndrome... Developmental delay, school, and speech problems are all part of this syndrome....Eric suffers from pathological rage attacks, as evidenced by his abnormal temper tantrums, breath-holding spells, and head banging. As he grew, he was unable to modulate his anger appropriately. He grew up with serious self-esteem problems... unable to ignore the teasing of other children... academic problems and difficulties with peers... low self-image....His family did not provide much in the way of intellectual challenges or psychological support. He grew up a lonely child, easily hurt...cried frequently...also developed a sadistic side...expressed in...cruelty to animals and... in his attack on Derrick Robie. At the time of that attack, however, I do not believe that Eric meant to kill the child. I believe that his rage overtook him. And he was completely driven by pathological anger, which was then out of control. Thus, I can say, with a reasonable degree of medical certainty, that the attack was not a premeditated murder but rather a tragic result of Eric's pathological rage."

During the trial, Dr. Herman will address the court and try to explain to the jury the psychological issues by which he feels Eric is affected.

"The mental illness which Eric had on that day definitely impacted on his anger and rage which was way out of proportion to any kind of provocation. At the time of the killing, his anger put him basically out of control so that he was so consumed with rage and anger he was not able to monitor himself or modulate his anger. He was not able to have insight into what he was doing at that moment in terms of what the end results would be. Eric was in an altered state of mind such that he could not understand, or take the time to appreciate what the ultimate result would be to his rage and anger. So, I don't feel that he was fully aware enough, nor could he stop himself at the time."

With the defense lawyer using psychiatric issues as a defense, the law requires Eric to submit himself for further examination by a health professional of the prosecutor's choice. They select Dr. Kathleen Quinn, a general child and forensic psychiatrist. As is usual with these sorts of cases, Dr. Quinn reads the reports of her peers. She determines Eric does not suffer from intermittent explosive disorder, but rather attention deficit hyperactivity disorder (ADHD), which she says was neither a major mental illness, nor an explanation for the killing.

Under cross-examination Bradley will divulge that Eric has bragged about the murder to inmates at the Detention Center. He even 'embellished' the account.

"Eric is a liar," says Bradley. "And he may very well have lied to me and he has lied in the detention center."

He hopes this will show Eric's actions are due to a mental defect, rather than the intent to kill.

13. FAMILY COURT DENIED

Despite allowing the battery of tests to take place, the prosecutor John Tunney refuses to consider any psychological or psychiatric evidence in making his decision that the case will not be heard in Family Court.

By order entered June 7, 1994, County Court denies Eric Smith's application for removal to Family Court. The court states it doubts it has the power to remove the indictment in the absence of consent by the District Attorney; nevertheless, the court considers the merits of Eric Smith's arguments in light of the statutory factors.

They conclude, because of the seriousness of the offence, the strong evidence of guilt, the need for such an act to be punished under the Penal Law, and the need for public scrutiny of the proceeding, this is not one of the 'rare' cases in which removal is warranted.

By way of explanation for his decision, District Attorney John Tunney says, "This isn't an accident of youth; this was a calculated act. I truly believe that Eric Smith is a budding serial killer."

Referring to Eric and his crime, the prosecutor makes it clear he believes Eric to be evil, not mentally ill. "There are clearly people who make choices which reflect pure evil. In—in my view, this heads the list."

When it is suggested by a journalist, "any thirteen-year-old who commits murder must be in some way nuts," the prosecutor replies, "I agree with you. That's not what's at issue here. Did he know what he was doing? Did he know when he was strangling Derrick that he was strangling a child, a person? And if he knew that what he was doing was wrong, that he shouldn't have been doing it, then he can have every psychological or psychiatric problem in the world, and he's still responsible for what he did."

14. INDICTED

On September 3, 1993, Eric Smith is indicted on a single count of murder in the second degree by a Steuben County grand jury. The definition of second-degree murder is any intentional murder with malice aforethought, but is not premeditated or planned. He is held at the Monroe County Children's Center in Rochester without bail.

The indictment is significant, as it means Eric Smith will not be given psychiatric help as his family had first thought, but would be prosecuted as an adult.

Many within Savona were relieved to hear the news, particularly Mary Davidson.

"It will allow the natural processes of justice and grieving to take their course," she said. "Prosecuting Eric as an adult is as it should be, and I'm extremely relieved."

Eric's lawyer, Kevin Bradley doesn't agree. He feels that as a child Eric lacks the mental capacity to understand the consequences of his actions. He wants Eric to be tried in a Family Court, where he will have his freedom in the future. If Eric is convicted in a Family Court he would be turned over to the state Division for Youth, which would place him in one of the four levels of institutions.

Bradley also believes a section of New York law may apply that protects juveniles from being tried as adults if their crime isn't part of a pattern and is not likely to be repeated.

Steuben Country District Attorney John Tunney dismisses both arguments. "The motion to move to Family Court would need my consent, and that's not going to happen. Nothing in the evidence suggests this crime was anything other than intentional. It was an intentional kill."

***

September 10, and Eric pleads not guilty to the second-degree murder charge. He comes before Judge Donald Purple in the Steuben County Court. Purple expresses concern about publicity affecting the trial.

***

In October 1993, Kevin Bradley asks for the suppression of Eric's oral and written statements to the police on the grounds the statements elicited were in violation of his Miranda rights, and were otherwise involuntary. The People oppose the motion and a Huntley hearing is conducted.

By order entered February 14, 1994, County Court denies Eric Smith's motion to suppress in all respects.

***

After attending all the preliminary hearings in Steuben County Court, Doreen Robie says of Eric, "There's not really much to think about. He just sits there in court and cracks his knuckles and looks out of the window. I've looked at him but he looks right through you. He just doesn't care what he did."

15. THE CONFESSION

With every child involved in crime, police have to be mindful of following procedure so as not to jeopardize the case, especially any confession elicited from the child. Questions will be asked much later in trials. Was the child coached, coerced, threatened into a confession? Was there an adult present? Did they understand their Miranda rights?

And so it was no different with Eric Smith. His lawyer, Kevin Bradley felt that the law enforcement officials had not followed protocol. By February 1994, Bradley was objecting strongly to the way in which the family of Eric were lulled into a false sense of security in believing Eric would be taken away to receive psychological help rather than being tried as an adult for first-degree murder.

Bradley feels too that Eric Smith deserved to have more explanations of the consequences of talking to a police officer than an adult would need.

Steuben County Judge Donald Purple ruled on February 18, 1994, that police had given Eric Smith ample warning that he had the right to remain silent and that he could have a lawyer present during his confession.

Judge Purple rules that the conversations between Smith and police before the teenager's confession were 'noncustodial in nature and voluntary...(and) in accordance with the requirements of the interview of minors.'

In addition, says Judge Purple, family members 'were aware that the defendant had the right to remain silent.' Further, he says, great-grandfather Carl Peters' role was 'protective' which was demonstrated when Peters ordered state police to stop questioning Smith early in the investigation.

16. THE TRIAL

By the time the case comes to trial it is August 2, 1994, a year to the day Derrick Robie was killed.

As the relatives of Eric and Derrick fill the front row of the courtroom, one empty seat separates both families. Derrick's grandfather, Jim Cook watches Eric enter the room and says to a family friend sitting behind him, "I wondered how I would feel the first time I laid eyes on him. I feel nothing. Absolutely nothing. It's amazing."

The People's direct case consists primarily of the defendant's confession. The primary defense is that Eric Smith lacks criminal responsibility by reason of mental disease or defect.

The trial opens with the six men and six women jurors, mainly blue-collar workers of middle-age with grown children, being shown graphic images of Derrick Robie's bruised body. They see images of the youngster with his pants pulled down to his knees, a bloody napkin stuffed in his mouth. They see too a twenty-six pound rock Smith had hurled at the preschooler's head.

As each member of the jury looks at the pictures, Eric Smith studies them closely.

One juror examines one of the photos longer

than the rest of her peers. As she passes the image to the next jury member, she looks across the courtroom at Smith and quickly averts her eyes.

The hushed court hears Roger Palmer's testimony. He describes the initial frantic moments after he discovers the body. He had been part of the search team that had combed the neighborhood looking for the young boy.

"Out the corner of my eye, I saw white," Palmer says. "I looked up, and that's when I saw Derrick. I noticed his shorts and underwear down, bruises, and a red object in his mouth."

Derrick's great-grandmother, Ruby Brownson, covers her face with her hands in anguish as a State Police crime scene technician identifies the stick that the Monroe County medical examiner removed from Derrick's body.

For the first time people hear Eric Smith's full confession as it is read out in court by District Attorney, John Tunney. Those present are stunned by the callous account.

On Sunday, August 1, 1993, I slept at my residence at 68 West Lamoka Avenue in Savona. I awoke at 7 a.m. and watched a few minutes of cartoons. My friend, Casey Monahan, aged 8, came over and watched cartoons with me. After a few minutes I got dressed and my mother took my twelve-year-old sister Holly to the dentist. Sometime after 7 a.m. Casey and I went to recreation. I was riding my Spalding, freestyle red bike. Casey rode Holly's pink-purplish small bike. I'm not certain, but I believe I was wearing cutoff blue jeans and my dark Harley T-shirt. I don't recall my shoes. I don't know what Casey was wearing.

We rode across West Lamoka Avenue to the Four Corners straight through the intersection and then turned right on Orchard Street. At the end of Orchard, we turned left onto McCoy. At the end of McCoy, we turned right to the recreation part to the pavilion.

There were three insurance people there. I had previously been told by Casey and others that they were insurance people. I asked the insurance people how long they would be there and they said until recreation starts. I don't know what time it was because I wear no watch.

Casey and I discussed going for a bike ride as we drove down to McCoy Street. As we turned left on McCoy, and in front of Farnsworth's house, we saw Jamie, Kim and Josh Carlton and another girl who I did not know. They were all walking towards the rec on Farnsworth's side of the street. I told the group that rec didn't start yet. They responded, 'Yeah, whatever.' At that time, Casey turned around and went back to the park with the group.

I continued up McCoy Street, and I think went for a bike ride, however, I can't remember what street. Shortly thereafter, I went to Monahan's house on 47

Church Street. When I got there, I saw Jamie Monahan, age 11, Pat Monahan, age 12, and the mom's boyfriend, whom I believe is named Casey. I did not speak to Casey as he was asleep in the mom's bedroom. I spoke with Jamie and Pat and asked about rec. Jamie said she would see me if she went. Pat was going fishing. Pat left the house first, and a few seconds later, I left.

Jamie was still at the house. I caught up with Pat on Church Street and we talked again about rec and fishing. Pat continued on Church, riding his bike which I believe is blue.

I turned right on McCoy and went directly to the park. I didn't see anyone when I arrived there. At the pavilion there were a few more insurance people and rec counselors, Kim King and Erica Ellison. A few seconds later, A.J., another counselor, pulled into rec with his dad's blue jeep. As I left rec, I turned onto McCoy Street and saw Mr. Randall in front of his house. As I waved to Mr. Randall, I looked left and saw a little kid with blond hair, a whitish T-shirt, carrying a bluish-brown bag with designs. He was walking towards rec on the sidewalk across from Mr. Randall's house on the downgrade. I turned around and went up behind when I was within ten feet, I said, 'Hey kid.' The kid turned around as I caught up with him. At that point, I knew I wanted to take him some place and hurt him. As I rode alongside the kid, I put my left sneaker on my front tire to keep the bike slow. I asked the kid if he wanted to go to rec by way of a shortcut through the weeds, then beat everybody there. The kid said, 'No, I am not supposed to.' I said, 'It's okay, I'm right here.' So (he) got in the middle of the empty lot between the yellow house with the white dog and the Farnsworth's grayish house. I turned to go into the weeds. The kid kept walking. I said to the kid again, 'It's okay I'm right here.' The kid then followed me through the empty lot. As the kid and I were walking to the corner of the empty lot near the Farnsworth's property line, the white dog from the yellow house was running back and forth on the cable run, barking loudly.

As we approached the 'fort-type area' I let the kid go in front of me. When we got inside the trees with the vine-type thing, I put my right arm around his neck. I was standing behind him. The kid then dropped his lunch. I continued squeezing harder as the kid made fists and swung his arms trying to get away. He hit me in the arms, but not very hard. He was also kicking his legs, and he kicked me in the shins. I was going to hold him against the tree and choke him with my hands. As I started to 'release' him he made a noise 'like he was trying to gasp air.' 'A weird noise.' So I said, 'Forget it,' and I squeezed harder. I let him go 'after 30 seconds or so.'

He didn't make any noise, so I let him down on the

ground. He was lying face up, with his arm up in a wave position, right arm down in an opposite wave position. His eyes were closed and I don't know if he was breathing.

There was a little rock lying beside him and I hit him in the head three times. I hit him on the right side of the head. I picked up a bigger rock, which was originally located about 18 inches from his head and partially buried. I pulled the rock from the ground and described it as possibly 15 inches by 10 inches and 6 inches thick. I also described it to Capt. DeLap as 'the rock with the most blood on it.' I threw the rock with both hands down onto his head. At this point, blood began running down his nose and the rock fell to the side. Two more times I picked up the rock and threw it onto his head for a total of three times. I then picked up another big rock but slightly smaller than the first, which was located 4 ½ feet from his left leg/knee. I threw that rock into the middle of his chest.

Now I remember that while he was lying on the ground, before I hit him with any rock, he was gasping for air. I dumped his lunch out onto the ground, which consisted of a sandwich, cookies, Kool-Aid, plastic reusable container and something else which I can't recall. Also, I saw a paper napkin, put it in his mouth. I pulled his chin down, put the napkin inside his mouth. I don't know whether it was over of under his tongue.

I then decided to also put the sandwich baggie in his mouth. As I tried to stuff the baggie in his mouth he bit me around my second knuckle, first finger, right hand. It hurt, but left no marks. I pulled my finger and the baggie out and threw the baggie down. I then began hitting him in the head with the rocks.

After the first time I hit him in the chest with the second large rock, I picked up the rock and dropped it on his chest again in the same general area. I then picked up the rock again and threw it into his midsection. At that point, I picked up the Kool-Aid and poured it on his face on the right side of his temple area, where I had hit him with the small rock, and on his chest.

At his point, I don't know whether I had pulled his pants down or not. However, I must have taken them down. I then looked around for a stick and picked one off the tree.

The tree was located toward the top and right side of his head. He was still lying on his back I believe the stick was skinnier than the pen used by Capt. DeLap and about 2 feet long. I then flipped him over and put the stick up his butt. There was approximately 6-9 inches sticking out. I think I put 1 ½ feet of the stick into him. I then flipped him back over, picked him up by the arm and hand and dragged him over to the rock pile. The rock pile was located 4 ½ feet to the right of the kid. I put him lying on his back, legs straight, left arm palm up and to the side and his right arm in a waving position. His head was facing left with the napkin still in his mouth. The napkin was soaked red with blood when I was done with him.

I then left the area the same as I had come as I had left my bike in the weed part of the lot. I rode out of McCoy Street and back to the park. After about five minutes at the rec, I went back to the body. I walked along the path alongside the baseball field on the path heading into the woods. When I got immediately adjacent to the body, I made a path to it. I was worried if he wasn't there he might say something.

However, I figured if he's dead, and I believed he was, I won't have to worry about anything. When I left the body, I went up through the brush onto the path in the middle of the brush. When I arrived back at rec, it started thundering and stuff, and Bill Horn the director, told everyone to go home. Casey and I left Lamoka on bikes and went to my aunt Clare Wilson's house on East Lamoka Avenue. At 11 or 10, I am not sure which, I called my mom and went home.

At no time did I sexually molest the kid, nor did I tell anyone until today that I killed him. The only ones I told today were my great-grandfather, Carl Peters, my grandfather, Gary Wilson, and my mother, Tammy Smith.

I know that what I did was wrong and I'm very

sorry for it.

As people listen to the confession they are frustrated by the lack of answers to the question, why? Why had Eric taken the life of another, and in such a brutal way? Why had he killed a boy he didn't even know?

Throughout the trial, the jury listens to a number of plausible reasons argued by each side as to why Eric Smith was driven to kill.

They hear that the possibility of his mother's use of drugs during her pregnancy contributed to leaving him with a rare disorder resulting in diminished responsibility.

The defense presents what they hope will be viewed as extenuating and contributing factors for Eric's behavior. They make it clear Eric comes from a dysfunctional family where his stepfather regularly subjected him to physical and mental abuse. He is a loner, not only bullied at home, but at school. Did the violence at home and the bullying at school cause him to lash out at the first thing that came his way?

Dr. Herman testifies that from an early age, Eric exhibited signs of emotional disturbance and sadism, a product of a family life in which there was "a significant amount of violence; verbal and physical."

Eric's stepfather, Ted Smith, he says, disciplined

the children by screaming and spanking. He also says Eric's sister, Stacy Hevner, now sixteen, left home to live with her father after her stepfather "sexually touched her twice"—acts of which Eric was aware.

"The methods used to discipline were extreme and would be terrifying to any child with the problem he had to grapple with," Dr. Herman says.

He agrees he cannot say with certainty the drugs Eric's mother took during her pregnancy had any bearing on Eric's behavior, but he says the undersized teen "has suffered from pathological rage attacks as evidenced by abnormal temper tantrums, breath-holding spells, and head banging. He grew up a lonely child who was easily hurt. He cried frequently," Herman writes in his report of May 1994, "As he grew, he was not able to modulate his anger."

While trying so hard to find the key to the behavior causing him to murder, Dr. Herman says Eric revealed to him he was urged to act when he saw young Derrick because of a 'mad switch'.

"It was the mad switch. I got mad. I got angry. I wanted to get it out."

"This was not a premeditated murder, but a tragic result of Eric's pathological rage," Herman continues.

Dr. Herman states the teenager suffers from

"intermittent explosive disorder", a condition characterized by discrete episodes in which a person loses the ability to control destructive impulses against others. The psychiatrist says Eric told him he selected Derrick as his target because "he's smaller and practically helpless."

He quotes Eric as saying: "I had to get my anger out on him. I wanted to hurt him."

Herman goes on to testify that other than the offer of the 'mad switch' Eric couldn't offer a reason for killing.

"He either knows, and he won't tell me, or he doesn't know."

Herman says that during his second interview with Eric, the teen took his legal pad from him and quickly drew a sketch of a character called Spike.

The drawing showed a man with a long head, a large chin, low-set ears and a cross-shaped earring in one ear. A cloud above the head said, 'Peace 2 U'. On the neck of Spike was a tattoo which read, 'I love Lucy.'

When Herman asked Eric to describe Spike he said Spike had friends, liked to go to college, listened to country music, was a friendly, soft-spoken person, had a brother named Tom, had a weird-shaped mouth and a father from Arizona called Carlos. Spike hates beer and has one enemy called 'Big Dog'.

"In a sense," explains Herman, "the character is

his idealized or positive image. Spike is everything Eric isn't. I think there is some meaning to it."

The defense further argues that a bizarre encounter with an insurance agent shortly before the murder could have been responsible for setting the plan into motion.

Eric came across a group of insurance agents sitting around a picnic table not far from where the summer camp was taking place. He hovers around the men and repeatedly bumps into the table with his bicycle.

He asks the men, "Is this where the kids meet?"

One burly agent, Thomas van Osdal from Elmira is present, and takes umbrage at the snarky question, but at this stage the conversation is still light.

He says to Eric, "I bet I can run faster than you can."

Van Osdol and Smith teasingly argue at that point. Van Osdol says another insurance agent begins taunting Smith. Van Osdol doesn't remember Smith's part of the conversation with the other agent because he is too stunned at what his colleague says next. He hears the man say, "I betcha I can beat your head in." Before anyone else can interject, the agent continues. "I betcha I have a gun in my glove compartment and I can shoot you."

Van Osdol says that at that point he quickly

escorts Smith away from the pavilion although Smith does not seem unduly upset by the ordeal.

Dr. Quinn, while denying Eric suffers from any major illness, when cross-examined, concedes on the day Eric killed Derrick, Eric would have been 'civilly committable' to a psychiatric hospital.

Quinn also states, "We are left with purposeful behavior by a boy who is comfortable and excited by aggression." Eric's behavior was 'purposeful' because he made rational choices such as moving the body to better conceal it, and because he indicated, he felt normal at the time of the killing, telling her he knew killing Derrick was wrong, and saying he had slept "like a baby" that night.

Pressed to explain why an apparently normal thirteen-year-old-boy would suddenly commit such a heinous offense, Quinn speculates Derrick Robie "may have been a very unusual or peculiar trigger who symbolized someone well cared for, and as a child successful, and competent, all the things Eric himself felt he was not."

Finally, and most importantly, from a legal perspective, Quinn testifies Eric was not under the influence of extreme emotional disturbance at the time of the killing and did not lack the capacity to appreciate the nature or wrongfulness of his act.

Throughout the testimony in Courtroom A, under the mint-green cupola of the Steuben County

Courthouse, Eric sits placidly, his face fixed in the same guileless expression since his implication in the crime, which has made it difficult to reconcile his depiction as a cold-blooded killer.

Doreen and Dale Robie reject the suggestion Eric is mentally incapable. They care little for the other explanations. They are not yet able to forgive Eric for what he did to their son.

"Something, I feel has to be done to him," says Dale Robie softly.

John Tunney knows how emotively charged the case is. He is desperate to secure justice for Derrick Robie. If the killer had been an adult, he knows his job would have been far easier. However, with the child a killer, he is worried the jury will be sympathetic. He urges the jury to stick to the facts when forming their verdict and not to be swayed by emotion.

"I suspect that there will come a time, when you · get in that jury room, you will be convinced that it has been proven that Eric intended to kill Derrick, that he is not criminally insane," Tunney goes on to caution the jurors of thinking that Eric Smith acted under extreme emotional disturbance. That would permit the jury to essential extend mercy to Eric, he tells them.

"As you evaluate that, ask yourself: Did Eric show Derrick Robie any mercy?" Tunney pauses and then says to hit home the point, "Forget it."

He tells the jury if a thirty-five-year-old man were sitting at the defense table, instead of a now fourteen-year-old boy, "you would be impatient to get into that jury room. He sits here sometimes dressed in cartoon characters, looking every bit the benign harmless child we want our kids to be. Our assumptions about children are destroyed by Eric Smith."

He also reminds them there is no doubt the intent to kill was there. Eric had intended to kill. His actions were calculated. When he returned to the crime scene he did so to make sure that Derrick was dead so he couldn't get up and tell on him. He also reminds them Eric Smith gave the authorities a detailed version of the attack down to the pattern on the paper towel he stuffed into the dying child's mouth.

"If Eric was in a rage, he would not have remembered such minutiae," Tunney states.

When Kevin Bradley takes the floor, he paces slowly before the jury, deep in thought, before launching his argument. Likewise, he urges jurors to dismiss sympathetic feelings when considering the case.

"Putting Dorie Robie on the stand—is that an appeal for sympathy? Is there any other reason for it?" he asks accusingly with a sly glance in Tunney's direction.

He says it should be clear to jurors Eric Smith suffers from a mental disease when he beat the four-year-old. He points out that Dr. Kathleen Quinn, the Cleveland psychiatrist, who testified for the prosecution, had been unable to say whether she agreed with defense psychologist Peter Cormack, who concluded that Smith 'becomes detached from his actions' during angry fits.

"That's an interesting answer," Bradley says. "Why can't she give an opinion?"

Dr. Herman, the Connecticut psychiatrist, said Smith suffers from periodic rage attacks he cannot control. Bradley tells jurors it is not necessary for the defense to prove Eric Smith suffers from a particular mental illness.

He goes back to criticizing Quinn's statement that because Eric seemed 'normal' to people before and after the murder, he was not in an altered state of mind at the time.

"The fact that he seemed normal afterwards, shows us that he's not normal!" Bradley says.

He asks jurors to consider whether it is more plausible Smith suffers from some mental disease that renders him incapable of understanding the consequences of his actions, or, as the prosecution suggests, a sadistic, jealous child who formed a plan to kill Derrick.

Bradley's summation of the case is punctuated by graphic descriptions of Eric's account of the murder. He uses drama in the courtroom to bring his point home. The lawyer picks up a twenty-six pound rock that is part of the evidence and holds it up in front of the jury.

"To pick this up, to throw this down on a little boy's head....Does this suggest a calm, deliberate action? A plan?" He repeatedly refers to Eric sodomizing Derrick with a stick. And he asks whether this defiling action was brought on by mental illness or an effort to 'skewering his insides'.

While Doreen Robie glares at her lawyer looking stunned and angry, she glances at her husband, and then closes her eyes, Bradley, like Tunney, urges the jurors to decide the case without emotion.

Attorney Kevin Bradley has a last attempt at rescuing his case. He asks Judge Purple to dismiss the second-degree murder charge, claiming District Attorney John Tunney has failed to prove it. Purple denies the motion.

Bradley then asks for a mistrial because of certain evidence that was admitted over his objections, and notably the emotional testimony of Doreen Robie, which he feels has jeopardized impartiality. Judge Purple denies that motion as well.

17. THE VERDICT

On August 16, 1994, the jury comes back into court to deliver their verdict.

If the jury concludes Eric is suffering from a mental disease or defect, or is under 'extreme emotional disturbance', it can result in a conviction of manslaughter. In that case, Eric will be confined for psychiatric treatment.

It does not take the jury of six men and six women more than ten hours to reject these claims and to reach a verdict shortly before 10 p.m. The jury rejects defense arguments that although Eric has a sadistic side, he is not criminally responsible because he suffers from 'intermittent explosive disorder', a rare condition characterized by episodes in which a person cannot control violent impulses.

The jury has weighed up the facts and found from the deliberate and calculating nature of the killing, and Eric Smith's attempts at concealment, he had a substantial capacity to understand and appreciate the nature and consequences of his conduct.

They focused on Eric's description of how and when he first saw Derrick, he 'knew he wanted to take him someplace and hurt him.' How he had repeatedly entreated Derrick to follow him through the woods until they had reached a place the defendant knew would be concealed from passersby. How he had tightened his chokehold, stuffed objects in the victim's mouth, and repeatedly bludgeoned the victim in response to the victim's "gasping for air." How subsequently, he left the scene for several minutes but returned to make sure the victim was dead. That conduct, felt the jury, reveals not only that Eric was in control of his actions, but that he also had a full understanding and appreciation of their nature and consequences. On this record, the jury is entitled to reject the defense of lack of criminal responsibility.

As the poll is taken, and each juror gives their answer, Doreen Robie's eyes fill with tears until the last juror has spoken. The only person to blame for the murder they say, is Eric Smith. Doreen breaks down and sobs.

"Thank you God, and tell DJ to go to sleep tonight," she whispers as the verdict comes through.

The jury finds him guilty of second-degree murder, meaning he intended to kill Derrick Robie after he saw him walking down the street.

The defense lawyer, Kevin Bradley asks for the minimum sentence of five years to life in the hopes the teen might avoid serving time in prison after the age of eighteen, if he "responds tremendously well to therapy."

Prosecutor John Tunney argues for the maximum term, suggesting it is up to prison authorities to decide when Smith is ready to be released. "To the extent that we're talking about rehabilitation, more is better," he says.

"Take the young man in to custody," Steuben County Judge Donald Purple says. The ginger-headed, freckled-faced boy shuffles out in his chains to a life behind bars, and his face shows not a flicker of understanding of the enormity of what has just happened.

Eric's parents are devastated. Stacy Hevner, Eric's older sister, wails as the verdict is read. Tammy Smith is so overcome by emotion Ted has to support her physically as they leave the courthouse. One of the great-grandmothers collapses in a hallway and an ambulance is called. However, neither parent readily admits they may be responsible for their son's actions.

Derrick's parents are just pleased the ordeal is finally over.

"I feel bad for some of his family," Doreen admits. "I know this is hard for them but they have to realize a funeral was harder for us."

When asked to describe her feelings towards Eric Smith she says, "You can't explain anything when it comes to this case."

"I think one of the bigger reliefs I felt from the

outcome was that maybe someone is starting to hold these kids responsible for their actions," says Dale Robie, afterwards. "We got what we came for. We thought, sooner or later, he would be held accountable. The verdict, however, will not bring Derrick back. All along we've been here for Derrick. We had to trust the system, and it worked. This is somewhat of an end. We can start going on from there."

***

For the jurors the trial has been harrowing.

Foreman, LeRoy Flint of Woodhull, Steuben County states, "We didn't feel he had an emotional defect or a disease. We felt there were emotional problems there, something of that nature, but we had to go with what the law read, which was extreme emotional disturbance. We took what we thought was presented as the facts, and we weighted them to the best of our ability."

He goes on to say there had been no immediate agreement among jurors, but added they did not have difficulty reaching a verdict. "We talked, we asked questions of each other, we worked on it, and we finally came to a solution."

Flint says the part that really touched him was when nine-year-old Casey Monahan was called as a witness and started crying in the courtroom. Eric had invited Casey to ride into the woods with him, around 9 a.m. on the morning of the murder but had refused the invitation. This was followed by a second young witness who too had turned down the same request by Eric, on the same morning. This witness clutched at his mother and sobbed as he left the courthouse.

"I have a seven-year-old daughter, and I can relate to them being scared, and that bothered me."

Asked what impact the case has had on him he replies, "It will be with me for quite a while. I don't think anyone will go away from this without being affected one way or another."

Another juror, Donna Ellis of Hornellsville, Steuben County, spoke with emotion. "I'm trying so hard to get my thoughts together," she says, her voice cracking. "I'm having an emotional low right now. It's one of the hardest things I've ever gone through."

For Mary Davidson, who owns the lot where Derrick was killed, she is at home when the news of the verdict comes through. As much as anyone, she is haunted by what happened to the young boy.

"It makes one look at what kind of society we live in where a child should kill another child. I was shocked it was a thirteen-year-old boy, a little sickened by it. We teach our children about strangers, but we don't teach them about other children that are playmates," she says.

On hearing of the conviction now, she is relieved, knowing that he's not going to be able to hurt any other child.

For the past year, Davidson has wrestled with the memory of the cries she dismissed as a cat's on that Monday morning, August 2.

"I don't think that'll ever go away."

***

A local journalist of Bath, Robert Lonsberry, has a column in the *Democrat and Chronicle*, a Rochester newspaper. He writes an article that appears in the paper on August 17, 1994, a day after the verdict that describes his observations and thoughts.

It's like Solomon. Not the good one. The one with the happy ending. It's like the other one. Where they cut the baby in half. It's justice, but it leaves you empty. Guilty. Guilty as hell. And everybody cried.

It's a small courtroom designed in a weird, curvy fashion. It turns in on itself and there are no straight lines.

No straight lines against which to measure anything. A crying mother on the left and a crying mother on the right.

And nobody wins.

The mother of the victim was comforted by her

husband, and the mother of the killer was comforted by her husband.

And nobody wins.

"This is the hardest part," defense lawyer Joe Pelych told the accused's parents two-and-a-half minutes before they learn their son's fate. "The next few minutes are the longest wait.

"This is the hardest part."

And two people sat there with the world looking at them pulled in on one another. The bailiff knocked on the door in the front on the left and a voice inside said, "They've reached a verdict."

And there is no hardest part.

It's all the same.

Hell doesn't have graduations.

It makes you sick to your stomach.

Two rows of small-town people in the middle of the madness and a jury of peers somberly walking to their seats.

The judge said some things and then he read the sheet and a little wave of muffled sobs rippled across the room.

Nobody wins.

A mother who lost her son last year went stiff and emotional and a mother who lost her son last night went limp and emotional. And justice seemed like a heartless business.

"Take the young man into custody," Steuben

County Judge Donald Purple said, and the circle came full.

It started in some weeds and it ended here, in the surreal world of lawyers and herding television cameras.

And justice seemed like a heartless business.

A thin wailing mother and her husband walking out the door. Out the door and into the future.

And you want to cry with them.

And it had nothing to do with the crime. It had to do with them and how wide a circle of destruction a few minutes of madness can wreak.

Madness, but not insanity.

Normal folks from this part of the world heard it and weighed it and decided it. And Eric is going away. And he seemed rock-like at the news. Standing and walking and looking down. Maybe dazed. Maybe like always.

And the judge adjourned and a weak lilting wail went up from beside the killer's mother.

Maybe it was a banshee and maybe it was a Valkyrie and maybe it was a breaking heart.

The county fair is going up across town. A big motionless Ferris wheel and strung lights and two boys who won't ever skip on a midway again.

It goes full circle, and it comes to an end.

And today the national cameras will leave.

This network and that network and they scurry to

cover then next freak of the week.

The world comes down here the last couple of weeks, to see what they could see.

It was an imperfect problem and an imperfect solution, and justice was done and that is important.

But when it happened, in the dark of the night in a town by the river, it just plain hurts.

It just plain hurts.

***

Kevin Bradley concedes Eric Smith has a 'serious psychological problem' for which he will not get help in a youth detention home or a state prison.

"My sense of it is that the kid has serious problems and that what you could have here is a serial killer." Bradley continues to say, "If you want to make one, this is a good way to do it."

John Tunney, the Steuben County district attorney says, "He's going to come back into society, and the last thing we want is an unaffected, unchanged Eric Smith back on the street. I do have confidence that he can be helped." Later, John Tunney will go on to say in a televised interview, he has no doubt Eric Smith would have gone on to become a serial killer, had he not been caught.

But the verdict further divides the community. They are divided, to some degree, by their relative closeness to either one of the two families. The fact that the horrific, brutal details of the crime are not made public knowledge also helps fuel the division by not knowing the full picture.

One woman, who requests anonymity, says she is frustrated by the conflicting emotions she feels.

"Some people say Eric needs another chance. My thought is, 'OK, how about next to your house, your kids?' On the other hand, I feel Eric is a victim, too."

"Basically, there were two murders," says Marlene Heskell. "Both of these kids have lost their lives, in different ways. And there's no one in town who doesn't feel for both families." She goes on to say, "Eric was a really complicated little boy, sweetness and venom. My heart kind of reaches out to him, but I also think, *How could you do this? You've hurt so many people.*"

Residents prided themselves on the village virtues of friendliness and concern. Yet they were blind to the darkness in their midst, oblivious to the growing turmoil raging inside the orange-haired boy. There is a feeling the community itself has somehow failed.

"Everyone says to themselves, 'What could we have done to prevent it? Why didn't we see the signs?'"

One neighbor of the Robies, who requests anonymity, says, "Maybe Ted Smith is the one who should really be on trial. There are a lot of people in town who feel that way."

18. SENTENCING

On November 7, 1994, Ted and Tammy Smith wait to hear the fate of their son.

They listen to Dale Robie as he gives his emotional victim statement. He pauses several times battling to regain his composure. Sometimes the pain and the sorrow are just too overwhelming and he stops to wipe the tears from his eyes. He tells them about his young son's short life and all the "firsts" he and his family will now miss.

"When Derrick came into this world I cried and when Derrick left this world I cried. I have felt the whole realm of loving and losing. Derrick didn't deserve to leave this world the way he did, but I'm proud of my son for the love he shared and the joy he gave to us all."

There is many a tear in the courtroom, just none from Eric Smith. All the while, with his future uncertain, listening to the bereft father talk about the loss of his son which he has caused, the now fourteen-year-old killer casts his eyes downwards but displays not a flicker of emotion. Not even after what he hears next.

"The person before you today took away all of what life had to offer Derrick and I pray that this person will never have the opportunity to take the life of another child."

The father returns to his seat and Doreen Robie, wiping away her own tears, tries to comfort her husband.

Kevin Bradley asks for forgiveness and to treat his client as a 'sick child' and not a 'younger version of an adult'. He also asks the judge not to send Eric away for life. He says, "Eric Smith is one of us, one of our children. He is a sick boy in need of treatment, not a 'thing', not a 'bastard', not a 'career criminal', not a 'bad seed', an evil child as those who are ignorant of the facts characterize him."

John Tunney focuses on Eric's attitude. He says he is bothered by the seeming lack of remorse Eric has displayed since his arrest and after his conviction.

As Judge Donald Purple reads Eric Smith's sentence from a prepared statement the previous day, Tammy Smith starts to cry. Eric is sentenced in Steuben County Court to nine years to life in a correctional facility.

Judge Donald Purple rejects Kevin Bradley's plea for leniency and a sentence with a fixed limit. Instead, Purple gives Eric Smith the maximum sentence allowed under the law for a juvenile defender.

Although Eric will receive credit for the time already served, the remaining years of his sentence must be completed before he becomes eligible for parole, which would not be before 2002.

Eric is to remain for the next two years in a state Division for Youth facility. On his sixteenth birthday he could be ordered to move to an adult prison, but by law, he could remain in the youth facility until the age of twenty-one. Although currently in Monroe County Children's Detention Center, the state has two weeks to move him to a Division for Youth facility.

Bradley comments on the decision afterwards. "It is very unusual to inflict a lifelong penalty on a child whose crime results from a very serious psychological illness that nobody knew about, with no opportunity to help," says Bradley. He says his client would be better served and helped in a youth facility. Here he could undergo successful therapy but if placed among adults in prison, all that would be undone.

"It hurts society for the court to make a decision today that no matter what happens to Eric in therapy and rehabilitation, he will still have to go to an adult prison."

Eric's parents cannot comment for as soon as they heard the sentencing they left in a hurry.

Kevin Bradley says they will appeal the sentence.

***

Eric Smith's sentence nine years to life is the maximum sentence possible for a youth convicted of murder under New York's 'juvenile offender' law. Both the conviction and sentence are appealed, but upheld by the appeals court.

19. A RETRIAL

By July 1997, Eric Smith has a new lawyer after Kevin Bradley excused himself from the case stating not only was he moving out of the area, but he had been ignorant of certain legalities and had not represented his client as well as he could have. He asked for a new trial and a new lawyer.

"Eric is a time bomb, and he's going to go off sometime," said Bradley. "If he's not getting serious individualized psychiatric therapy in the prison setting, then nobody's being helped, particularly society. All I'm trying to do is put Eric in a mental institution where he can stay for the rest of his life."

The new lawyer was the well-known Felix Lapine from Rochester. He concurred with his colleague Kevin Bradley that he had failed his client by not knowing enough about the insanity defense, and in addition, had made some egregious errors at trial.

He went on to tell Judge Donald Purple, "Mr. Bradley marched Eric into the jaws of death."

Judge Purple said he would re-look at the facts and give his ruling on whether there was recourse for a new trial.

Within a month, Judge Purple had his answer ready. There would be no new trial.

In a five-page document outlining his decision Judge Purple said that Kevin Bradley had provided adequate legal representation for his client. "The allegations of ignorance of the law and ineffectual counsel are without merit," he said.

When asked how he felt about the ruling, Felix Lapine said he was not surprised to hear the ruling, for if it had been any otherwise, it would have meant the judge himself had been at fault. He did say, however, he would take his client's case to the Appellate Division all the way to the US District Court if need be to get justice he felt his client deserved.

20. PSYCHOLOGICAL TREATMENT

The Smith family and Eric's lawyers are shocked and disgusted at the fourteen-page treatment plan the Brookwood Center, a Division for Youth facility for boys aged thirteen to twenty-one, has put together for Eric in December, 1994. His parents refuse to sign the plan and, in turn, they are told the implementation of the program does not need their consent to proceed with the proposed action.

According to mental health specialists at the Brookwood Center, Eric needs extensive psychological treatment for his "sexually offending behavior and thoughts."

"I was shocked by the plan. It's rubbish," retorts Ted Smith. "I can't believe any of it. He needs help, but he needs the right help. And if he doesn't get it who's to say what might happen?"

The report goes on to say, "Smith liked killing his victim and liked talking about it. Eric stated he did this to get it off his chest."

Kevin Bradley and Ted Smith say Eric never told anyone he enjoyed the murder.

The report says the killing was sexually motivated because Eric suffers from necrophilia—an erotic fascination with dead bodies.

"None of the four doctors who examined him in connection with the court proceeding said this was a sex crime," says Bradley.

Ted explains why he and Tammy refuse to sign the treatment plan. "There are just too many things wrong with it." To highlight why they think this he references an inclusion from the report that Smith is allergic to shrimp and clams. He says, "I don't think my son's ever eaten them. How could they know that he's allergic to them? It scares me because it's just a taste of what they will do to him. I don't think they're going to help him."

21. WANTING A SECOND CHANCE

Eric Smith's first parole hearing comes up in 2002. As he was given nine years to life, there is a possibility he could be back in Savona with his family if his hearing is favorable.

The Robie family is sent a notification letter by the parole board, giving them four days to prepare a letter contesting Eric's potential release.

When his parents are asked about their contact with Eric, Ted Smith reflects on whether his treatment of him as a child or the bullying at school are contributing factors to what happened. He goes on to say he and his wife visited Eric regularly while he was in a Rochester area juvenile detention center. Financial and health reasons have since prevented them from traveling over the last year to Dannemora to their son after he was moved after eight years.

Eric is now in the Clinton Correctional Facility, a maximum security state prison in Dannemora, near Plattsburgh. He was moved on his twenty-first birthday, on January 22, 2001.

Ted Smith says, "Eric calls us several times a month. He's like he's always been. He's always been our kid."

Eric Smith has to be transferred to a special cellblock for inmates with disabilities after he is savagely beaten when he first enters the prison system in 2001.

"He's just a little guy—about five feet, four inches tall, and about 125 pounds. And with his red hair and glasses and the way he looks, he gets picked on by the other prisoners," says Ted.

Ted admits he cannot recall Eric ever apologizing to his family or the Robie family for the grief he inflicted. "But he said he started thinking about it for the first time a few months ago. He's finally starting to feel some emotion."

Eric hasn't spoken with his parents about the upcoming parole hearing but Ted says, "I'm pretty sure he would like to be paroled. I don't think they're going to give it to him, but sure, he would like to be out of prison. Anybody would."

When John Tunney is contacted, he says he has received reports of Eric's behavior in prison that "indicate he remains a dangerous person." He says, "Those reports don't give me any reason to believe he has any real insight into his own conduct or the reason he killed" and reveals, he has "no empathy for the victim or his family."

Tammy Smith says, "All I pray for is that he gets the help he needs so that this will never happen again."

She also issues a statement directed in part to the Robie family: "I want everyone who has gone through this terrible tragedy, especially the Robie family, to know that our entire family feels so terrible this happened at all. Our family will never be able to express, or put into words, the loss or ongoing pain but we want you to know that we all hope for you and your family peace and serenity someday."

Ted Smith says that like the Robie family and others in the community, "My wife and me, and everybody else that knew Eric, has been affected by what he did. If anybody in the world understands why this happened they're way ahead of us. Not even Eric understands it. He just knows he did something horrible."

When it comes to Eric Smith's parole request, he says he has changed. "My thoughts are not the same. My values are not the same. I don't look at life as some menial thing. It was pretty much he was in the wrong place at the wrong time. With the mentality that I had, I didn't care about life. I didn't think my life was really worth anything from the way people reacted to me and the way I was treated."

He goes on to say how he had been bullied because of his hair and his looks and how initially he had taken out his anger on animals. He also attended a sex-offender treatment program he says, that has helped him a lot.

"I don't believe in, you know, the things that I

used to believe in...hurting people mainly. I thought that I had the power to do it, and power does not come from taking life, it comes from giving and helping and I didn't learn that until later."

The parole board Commissioners Robert Dennison and Patricia Tappan deny his application. "This was a horrendous criminal act and you appear to have little remorse for your young victim. Your positive institutional adjustment was taken into consideration by this panel. However, to release you at this time would deprecate the seriousness of your vicious criminal act and undermine the respect for the law. We also feel that there is a strong and reasonable probability that you would commit additional criminal acts and endanger the welfare of society."

Eric Smith will remain in prison for another two years. His next parole hearing is scheduled for June 2004.

***

In the same year as Eric's first parole hearing, the Robie family joins the fight for the passage of 'Penny's Law'. The law is named Penny Lae Brown, a thirty-nine-year-old Salamanca woman who was raped and murdered by a fifteen-year-old teenager in 1999.

As part of her lobbying effort, Doreen Robie testifies in May 2002, in Rochester, before a panel of New York State Assembly Republicans. People listen and the legislation increases the mandatory sentence for juveniles convicted of second-degree murder in New York from five to nine years to life, to fifteen to twenty-five years to life.

***

In 2004, after elven years in prison, Smith, aged twenty-four, admits his family life was abusive and as devastating as the bullies who taunted him at school. However, Smith insists neither his stepfather Ted nor anyone else sexually abused him.

He tries to explain why he killed Robie but his explanations fall short. Smith does not take ownership of his crime, referring to himself as if he were speaking for other people using terms such as *the individual* and *they*.

He tells the parole board he killed Derrick Robie because he was scared of being caught not because he felt bad. He said he only started to feel remorse much later.

Commissioner Gino Nitti asks Eric, "If you had not admitted to someone that you had done this, do you think it would be a fair statement to say that you probably would have done this again?"

"Yes," he answers.

Asked why he had sodomized Derrick with the stick his response is that when he had done it he had not felt sexual gratification by the act. He had done it to cause internal bleeding and to improve the chances the boy would die.

When listening to his delivery of events it is still flat and devoid of emotion. Not once does he show real remorse or a connection to the child whose life he ended as heartlessly as he did with the snakes or Sammy the cat.

Only once does he mention Derrick by name. There is no true remorse for his actions more than a decade later, just a half-hearted explanation for the crime. The delivery is clinical, methodical, lacking in human empathy and introspection.

The reference to 'the kid' distances himself from the awful events that took place solely at his own hands. These are disturbing signs Eric Smith has not truly repented and perhaps never will.

The parole board is not convinced Eric has made sufficient progress during his incarceration. "You freely admitted that if you had not been arrested for this crime that you would be capable of killing again. We believe that to have been the case then, and now."

Board members go on to report Smith shows "a lack of insight and understanding as to what type of person you were, and indeed continue to be, ever so many years beyond this terribly brutal crime."

He is denied parole. "Despite your lengthy incarceration to this point, this panel is of the opinion that should you be released at this time, you would continue to pose a clear and present danger to the safety and welfare of society. Your release would pose an unreasonable and unacceptable risk to the safety and welfare of others."

He is eligible for parole again in June 2006.

***

In 2006 Smith says, "I would like the opportunity to re-enter society, not because I feel I've done enough time, but I want an opportunity to help someone not commit a crime the way I have, or help young kids coming into their teenage years."

Smith tells the parole officials if he has the opportunity to study forensic psychology he can talk to teenagers who are having emotional problems and warn them if they do not get help, they too could end up in jail.

"I am not going to go out into society and commit another crime, because I know what would happen if I went out and violated in any way, minor or major. I know I would never have the opportunity to re-enter society again."

Smith admits to the board the anger he felt in

1993 led to the attack on Derrick Robie.

"There's really nothing I can say to diminish it. I know it was a serious crime. I've taken responsibility for it. I wish I had never committed this crime. I do regret it. I have remorse for the victim and the victim's family."

Asked during the hearing whether he would have attacked a person who was six feet, four inches tall and weighed 200 pounds, Smith replies, "It depends if I had something to overpower him with."

The board denies his application. However, this denial draws criticism from Smith's lawyer, Susan BetzJitomir of Bath. BetzJitomir is Smith's latest attorney, a mother of five and a former college professor, graduating four years ago from Cornell Law School and whom Smith pays $5 a month for her services.

She files an appeal on October 10. In the document she says the board's decision "was in part arbitrary and capricious and violated Mr. Smith's due process rights, resulting in harsh and excessive punishment."

BetzJitomir's appeal argues the board improperly considered two incidents in which Smith was involved: "A remote in time" consensual kiss with another inmate, and a behavioral violation the lawyer says, "amounted to not putting out a cigarette fast enough."

BetzJitomir says with the exception of those two

incidents, "Eric has been a hard-working, no-problem prisoner. He is a mild-mannered, hard-working, well-read inmate who has completed a sex offender program."

Eric says he wants to return to Savona and live with his mother and his stepfather if he is released.

Doreen Robie says the family has always feared Smith's release back into the tiny community. "It would be life-changing for our family, which I don't think would be fair," she says. "We would have to leave, unfortunately."

The parole board states in June, Smith's release would be "incompatible with the welfare of society."

***

In 2008 Eric Smith is twenty-eight years old. He goes before the three-member panel at the Orleans Correctional Facility near Albion. In the panel are Walter William Smith, Patrick Gallivan and Gerald Greenam III.

Again, he tells the board he is ready to help troubled teens. He feels he is qualified because, "I'm understanding (sic) of what they're feeling because I felt it."

Smith admits in the hearing he tortured animals as a youngster and that his slaying of four-year-old Derrick Robie may qualify as 'torture'.

"What are some of the things you would do to the cats?" a parole commissioner asks.

"Usually drown them."

"And...what other things did you do besides drowning?"

"I ran over them with a four-wheeler."

When asked why he had used an all-terrain vehicle to run over cats his comment is, "I never learned how to drive a car."

Asked whether his slaying of Derrick Robie could be called torture, Smith answers, "I am not really qualified enough to know."

Later, the commissioner presses the question, likening Eric's killing of animals to his willingness to fatally brutalize the four-year-old.

"Don't you think that both of those instances are torture?"

"Yeah, to an extent," Smith replies.

Smith points out he has had no violent incidents while incarcerated during the past fifteen years and his disciplinary record is spotless. He again speaks of wanting to take college-level courses in forensic psychology and possibly child psychology.

He tells parole commissioners he thinks he 'would be an asset to society' if he were released.

His application is denied with the following comment released by the board: "This panel remains concerned with a mindset, which, for no legitimate reason, would cause you to brutally and savagely beat and sodomize an innocent four-year-old child. This senseless disregard for the sanctity of human life and the norms of our society continues to raise questions about your ability to lead a law-abiding life. When considered with required and relevant factors, it is concluded that your discretionary release at this time remains incompatible with the welfare of the community."

***

In 2010 Eric is given yet another chance at a bid for freedom. He tells the board he has learned how to deal with his anger and how to express it in more constructive ways. He is no longer disrespectful to others. He has learned how to be assertive even in uncomfortable situations. He has values and morals, things he did not have, he says, at the age of thirteen. He has also learned to appreciate life.

The board notes Eric has a clean disciplinary record, and he obtained his GED (General Equivalency Diploma) in 1999. He has also trained as both a carpenter and an electrician. He says he is looking forward to being employed if paroled.

When asked if he would like to add anything additional to the hearing he says this: "I know that given the opportunity to re-enter society I know I'm not going to hurt anybody. I'm not a threat, and I'd like the opportunity to try and live a life even though I'm in here for taking one. I can't change it. If I could, I'd do it in a heartbeat without question and I'd really appreciate it if I can get that opportunity to not only prove to you, but to prove to myself that I'm worth it. I know I am, and I'd like the opportunity."

The parole board is unswayed by his answers. They make the following decision: "If released at this time there is a reasonable probability you would not live and remain at liberty without violating the law. Your discretionary release at this time would so deprecate the seriousness of the crime as to undermine respect for the law. Based on all required factors in the file, discretionary release at this time is not consistent with public safety."

***

Again, in 2012, aged thirty-two, Eric's case comes up for revision. He admits for the first time he had been abused. He does not specify what type of abuse he suffered.

"I was always targeted and me feeling uncomfortable and vulnerable and powerless I shut down emotionally and that caused me to be insensitive to human life."

He goes on to say he understands why he has

been denied parole for the last five times. He just wasn't ready. However, now he believes he is. He knows he still has "work to do" and understands the "value of life."

"I understand that in the nineteen years that I've been incarcerated, I realize that had I been released earlier, I wouldn't have been ready because I wasn't emotionally connected."

However, the board is still unconvinced. His release "is not presently warranted due to concern for the public's safety and welfare. It would not be compatible with the welfare of society at large, and would tend to deprecate the seriousness of the instant offense, and undermine the respect for the law."

Eric's lawyer says Smith had been "a model prisoner" and has spent more time in prison than most adults who commit murder.

"It's shocking and appalling that he is still in there," complains his lawyer, Susan BetzJitomir. "He's no more harm to society than anyone who didn't commit a crime as a child."

She does acknowledge, however, the notoriety of his crime has not helped his chances. "People don't want to be blamed if something happens," she says of the parole officers who decide whether they should set Smith free.

***

Eric Smith, in 2014, is in the maximum-security Collins Correctional Facility in Erie County, about twenty-five miles south of Buffalo.

He is now thirty-four, and tells the Parole Board on April 11, 2014, he was angry, had been abused by family, and bullied by classmates so he took his frustration out on four-year-old Derrick Robie.

"He didn't deserve anything that I did to him; no one deserves that kind of violence," Smith says. "What I did to him was brutal."

Smith admits he is responsible for Derrick's death and is remorseful for "what I've done to him and his family."

Smith tells the Parole Board when he was thirteen he did not trust anyone and felt everyone was out to get him.

"I took my anger and frustration and rage out on him," Smith tells the board, and explains those emotions weren't directed at Derrick, but at his father, older sister and the high-schoolers who bullied him. "I took it out on (Derrick) and he did not deserve that."

According to the transcript, Smith says he killed Derrick because he thought he would get into trouble if the boy got up and told on him. He claims he thought by inserting a stick into the boy, it would reach and "stop his heart."

Smith describes his own actions as "horrendous," "violent," "uncalled for and wrong." He tells the board he believes he is not a threat to others as his values have changed and he has stayed out of trouble while incarcerated for nearly a decade.

"Who I was at age thirteen does not exist," Smith says. "That child that committed that crime, he's gone. He's never coming back."

Parole officials feel Smith appears to be making progress in institutional programs and has a clean discipline record. Nevertheless, they deem his release "incompatible with the welfare and safety of society."

For the seventh straight time Smith faces a three-member Parole Board and again he is denied his freedom.

***

In 2016, aged thirty-six, and for the eighth time, Eric Smith's case is reviewed. This time there is no transcript, nor any evidence to show he spoke at this hearing. After looking at his case file and all the reports, and after careful consideration, the parole board view him as still being too dangerous to be let back into society. His application is denied.

***

Eric's last parole to date takes place in April 2018, at age thirty-eight. His application is again denied.

Smith says he might not have fully realized what he had done when he killed Derrick Robie all those years ago. However, after taking part in a special program, he now feels remorse.

"I don't think I fully understand or understood at the time, the full impact of who I was hurting. I was aware of the fact that I was hurting Derrick Robie at the time, but I wasn't thinking about the effects it would have on his mother and father; his younger brother," Smith says.

"I realize that I took a little boy who deserved to live in every possible way, shape and form. Whether he grew up to experience a lot of bad or a lot of good, he still should have had that right to do that and I took that away," Smith tells the parole board.

The parole board returns a decision not to release Eric Smith due to concerns of public safety. While Smith has participated in "positive programming" while incarcerated, volunteers with the chaplain, and has repeatedly apologized for his actions, "it does not outweigh the severity of your brutal crime."

However, this time the three-member commission is not unanimous in their feelings towards Eric's continued incarceration.

In a dissenting opinion, one member says after twenty-four years in prison, Smith is now a mature adult who accepts responsibility for his actions. Further incarceration serves no purpose.

He will be eligible for parole again in 2020. With a lack of a unanimous vote at his last parole hearing, Smith is more hopeful than ever that he could be released soon.

22. STILL LOOKING FOR ANSWERS

Ted Smith was a broken man after the trial. The baseless rumors of his sexual abuse of Eric, and the acknowledgement of the inappropriate fondling of his stepdaughter ended up with Ted losing his job at Westinghouse.

People could neither forgive nor forget. John Di Crasto says after the murder the Smith family received a lot of hate mail. One person leaves particularly vicious notes on the windscreen of Ted's truck. Ted thinks he knows who the person is. He finally finds him sitting in his truck in a car park with binoculars trained on the Smith house. Ted comes up from behind, reaches in, and slams the individual's head against his own steering wheel. The letters stop after that.

After both parents lose their jobs Ted finds himself in great financial difficulty. The strain and stress are contributing factors to his death when he suffers a heart attack and passes away on Monday, June 18, 2007. He is only forty-six-years-old.

John Di Castro is devastated when Ted Smith dies as he was a good friend to John. They met through cars and mechanical work, Ted being a mechanic and John a welder. Ted Smith, portrayed by the media as a hard man largely to blame for

Eric's behavior, is not the man John Di Castro knew. He describes Ted Smith as a gentle giant, a warm, tenderhearted man, but a no-nonsense sort of man. A man whom Di Castro admits physically disciplined his kids, but those who criticized allowed their kids to run wild.

People had helped spread false rumors Ted had sexually molested Eric. Ted changed after the murder and became an emotional wreck. He was well-liked by those who knew him and John recalls Ted Smith's funeral being 'a full house'. He goes on to say, "That horrible stigma followed him. He was on the news several times and I don't think that helped him. Notoriety made things worse for him. Time does not go on that I don't feel the loss of a good friend. Everyone was hurt in one way or another. I am sure many would like to forget the whole deal. I can never forget it, and if I can make a stand for Ted, then I would be as good a friend to him as he was to me."

***

The Robies, other victims' families and state lawmakers have urge the state Legislature to pass a bill that would require violent felony offenders to wait five years, instead of the current two years, between parole hearings.

Supporters say the measure would alleviate the

grief families of victims have to go through every two years before the parole board.

"With current laws in place, families such as ours re-live every two years the heartache of our loss," Dale Robie says at a news conference near the state Capitol. The bill has support in the Republican-led Senate, but has faced resistance in the Democratic-led Assembly. Advocates say there has been a concern from some lawmakers that the measure could provide a disincentive for violent felons to rehabilitate.

"This is about the victim. It's about the victim's family that has to relive this nightmare every other year, going through the parole process," O'Mara agrees. "It's not right. It's not fair."

The bill which passes the Senate in 2015 could increase the time between parole hearings to five years. It has been updated in the Senate to only include those convicted of Class A felonies. Supporters are hoping this amendment will be passable within the Assembly soon.

**

Still today, the ultimate question goes unanswered. Why did Eric Smith kill Derrick Robie?

Smith's attorney, Susan BetzJitomir believes Smith should be released. "The issue isn't what kind of disturbed child was he then," says BetzJitomir.

"The question now is what kind of young man is he now? Because that's the question the parole board faces."

She credits the enormous change she sees in Smith to the intensive counseling he received during the six years he was held at Brookwood Juvenile Detention Center. Smith was transferred to Clinton Correctional Facility, an adult prison, when he turned twenty-one. Currently, Eric resides in Gowada Correction Facility in Erie County, NY, a medium security facility.

To demonstrate he has changed, BetzJitomir allows Eric to read a statement he has prepared. But she does not permit him to answer any questions.

"I know my actions have caused a terrible loss in the Robie family. And for that, I am truly sorry," says Smith. "I've tried to think as much as possible what Derrick will never experience; his sixteenth birthday, Christmas, anytime, owning his own house, graduating, going to college, getting married, his first child. If I can go back in time, I would switch places with Derrick and endure all the pain I've caused him. If it meant that he would go on living. I'd switch places, but I can't."

John Tunney's response? "I don't doubt that somewhere along the line, a light bulb has gone on. And all of a sudden, Eric has a better understanding of the enormity of what he did," says Tunney. "Does that mean he's now safe to be back among us? Of course not!"

Reflecting on his troubled childhood, Smith again describes the intense pain he endured at the hands of bullies. "So after quite a few years of verbal abuse, and having been told that I'm nothing, I shut down my feelings. So I wouldn't feel the emotional pain, which made me vulnerable and weak. But the damage was done."

Smith adds, "I began to believe that I was nothing and a nobody. And my outlook on life was dark. I felt that when I went to school, I was going to hell because that's what it was for me."

BetzJitomir says Smith had no friends at school, "Nobody liked him."

At this point, Smith has come as close as he ever has to answering the question that has haunted so many people for so many years. Why did he do it?

"However minor or major each abuse situation, it all adds up. Until it gets to the point where the individual cannot take anymore," says Smith. "After a while, they may cope in a horrific way or take their emotional anger or rage out on someone who had done nothing to bring on such violence like Derrick. Not because they're evil or satanic little kids. It's because they want the abuse to stop. And it's the only way they know how to."

But Tunney points out Smith had given the parole

board a more chilling explanation for the killing. When asked if killing Robie gave him a good feeling, Smith says, in a transcript of the interview, "At the moment, it did, yes." When asked why he did it, Smith says, "Because instead of me being hurt, I was hurting someone else."

Smith talks more about what he believes drives children to kill and suggests he was abused at home. "Although each case is different, there is always the underlying fact that the kids who did, who do these unthinkable crimes endure years of abuse. Whether at school, at home, or both, I had issues at home. But I'm not going to talk about that."

Eric has made the case he is uniquely qualified to counsel bullied children, and one day sees himself as a forensic psychologist, doing research on children who kill.

"I think society might be safer if he were allowed out to do that kind of research," says his attorney. "Because nothing will change what happened to Derrick. But maybe something can prevent what might happen to someone else's child."

Tunney, however, disagrees. "Let's assume he's not a threat anymore. OK. Should we release him? There's a lot more to talk about. That is, has he been punished enough?"

Kevin Bradley sums up the enigma of the case. He says, "Frankly, a lot of questions about Eric have not been answered. This is the kind of case where questions can be asked forever."

Those looking for answers as to why Eric Smith actually killed Derrick Robie, and why he has been so unsuccessful in securing his freedom, could be found in the words of District Attorney, John Tunney.

"He could have just killed Derrick. But he chose not to. Eric continued to deal with Derrick's body because he wanted to, because he chose to, and most frighteningly of all, because he enjoyed it."

THE END

AFTERWORD

It would appear that lawyers, attorneys and judges are fallible too. In the author's research she came across two court cases against two of the prominent legal men in the Eric Smith case.

The first was Eric Smith's defense attorney, Kevin Bradley, who in April 1996, was in trouble for slapping his thirteen-year-old daughter on Easter Sunday.

He was arrested and charged with third-degree assault and endangering the welfare of a child, after his daughter reported him to school authorities, who in turn reported the incident to the police. Bradley's lawyer was none other than Joseph Pelych.

According to Pelych's business partner, David Coddington, the incident had involved disciplining a child and that the charges had been 'trumped up'.

In the end, the case was dismissed through lack of sufficient evidence.

"There was no physical injury under the law," said Judge Tantillo. "The law allows parents to use reasonable force in disciplining a child."

The second court case occurred in relation to an incident that took place on April 28, 1996. Judge Donald Purple had been at the Elks Club that Sunday and had had one too many drinks. As he left the Elks Club in Corning he pulled out of the parking lot and struck a parked vehicle before accelerating off the road and hitting a tree in the yard next to the club.

With a head injury he was taken to the emergency

room at the local hospital, but refused to take a blood test at the time. Lt. Hugh. J. Simmons of the Corning Police Department said that it was clear that the judge was intoxicated.

If convicted of reckless driving and driving under the influence he faced two years in jail. However, in June he pled guilty to driving while intoxicated, was fined $500 and had his license suspended for six months.

Judge Purple retired April 1, 1998, and moved to Charleston, South Carolina to be closer to family. Although only sixty-three, he said he had suffered ill-health due to a heart problem, and that this was the reason behind his retirement.

CHAPTER PREVIEW BOOK 3: KIDS WHO KILL - CRISTIAN FERNANDEZ

1. TOXIC FAMILIES, DAMAGED LIVES

Babies are born every day. There are those who are wanted, fussed over, cared for, loved, and brought up in nurturing and safe environments. Then there are *the others*; those misfortunate ones some consider 'disposable'. They are the unwanted, the unloved, the neglected. They become a target for physical, psychological, and sexual abuse. The latter becomes the unfortunate fated lives of Biannela Marie Susana and her young son, Cristian Juan Fernandez.

Biannela Susana's first eight years in the Dominican Republic, the country of her birth, are happy ones, despite being the product of a broken home. Her parents divorce when she is two. By the time she is six, she is living with her grandmother who showers her with love and bakes her three-tiered birthday cakes. Biannela's biological father lives right across the street, allowing him to see his daughter often, which he does, and enjoys such activities as teaching her to swim.

Sonia Valdez, the young girl's mother, is largely absent, with long periods passing between visits. Months soon turn into years. Biannela's life is about to turn upside down, when Sonia returns unannounced and informs her parents she has come to fetch her daughter to live with her in Miami, Florida.

Biannela, torn from a stable environment, arrives with an estranged mother to a strange country, knowing no one, and struggling with a language she does not understand.

During her pre-teen and teenage years, unlike those spent with her loving grandparents, Biannela's mother is emotionally disconnected. Not only that, she severely neglects her daughter's basic needs. She does not show her much in the way of positive care, nor does she provide supervision of her daughter's safety. Sonia Valdez's parental skills are hampered further with significant issues of substance abuse for she is a heavy drinker, abusive, and often throws crockery and other objects while in a rage. In addition, she has a cocaine habit.

When Biannela is ten, her mother forgets to pick her up from school. The young girl rushes out of the building and soon the yard empties. Shadows lengthen until they meld into dusk. Her little heart quickens and fear rises. Overwhelmed, she starts to cry, for it is well after dark and still her mother has not fetched her. Eventually, a passerby notices the girl and calls the police. When the officer asks Biannela where she lives, she cannot remember the name of the motel at which they are staying; the family has moved that many times.

Together with a new stepfather, who is eleven years her mother's senior, the family moves from place to place living in cheap hotels, motels, trailer parks, and camping in the homes of strangers. The relationship between her mother and the new husband is volatile. There are often violent outbursts and the young girl witnesses physical altercations between the two. At no time does Biannela feel loved or wanted. Instead, her mother is demeaning, and the child is largely left to raise and fend for herself.

The pattern of neglect and the transient lifestyle culminates in the next episode of Biannela's tumultuous life that will be life-changing for the young girl.

Sonja Valdez finds work at a landscaping business, and after school, Biannela goes to the company's office and waits for her mother to finish her shift. In the afternoons the office is empty, occupied by the lonely, now eleven-year-old little girl, who is trying hard to complete her homework. She finds school difficult. Not only is there no parental encouragement in her scholastic achievements, she also has an IQ of 86.

Working at the same landscaping company is nineteen-year-old José Antonio Fernandez. While Biannela is alone in the office, José stops by and befriends her. His visits become more frequent until he asks Biannela's mother if the young girl can sleep over at his house as he has a daughter living with him that could do with some company. Her mother only too willingly agrees.

Biannela's trips to José's house become more and more frequent. She would later say about him, he was the first person since her grandmother who made her feel special. As a result, she was willing to do whatever he wanted.

It is not too long into the relationship when Biannela falls pregnant. She is still only eleven years old. José sees the signs and demands she has an abortion. Biannela knows her mother will want the same thing. It is not what Biannela wants. She wants to keep it. With a baby, she knows she will not be alone anymore. She will finally have someone she can love, and who will love her in return.

So she hides her thickening waist from her mother by wearing baggy clothes until one day people start talking and suggesting to her mother the girl is pregnant. By the time her mother takes her to the doctor for an examination, it is too late for an abortion.

The squalling baby enters the world on January 14, 1999, in Miami, Florida. His mother is now twelve, going on thirteen. José Fernandez, now twenty, is charged with statutory rape and given ten years' probation. He escapes jail time by telling the judge he hopes to help raise his son. He is also required to be registered as a sex offender.

He does not, however, accept any responsibility for his actions and impregnating someone too young to understand consensual sex. Instead, he puts the blame on Biannela. He claims she told him she was sixteen, and he had no idea that she was just eleven. He also says, "She would come around to find me...she would not leave me alone. (I was giving her the) love and affection that she didn't get from her mother."

As soon as Cristian is born, Biannela's mother refuses to allow her to go back to school. Instead, she expects her daughter to be a full-time mother. As the family continues to move, the young girl has no friends and is left to her own devices to care for the newborn as best she can. However, with a poor role model, her parenting skills are minimal.

At fifteen months old, Cristian is hospitalized with pneumonia and is there for five days. She is recorded as being thirteen years old, the baby's primary caretaker, and still not in school. She is living with her mother who works from 8 a.m.–10 p.m. The baby has not seen a pediatrician since he was two months old, and his vaccinations are not up to date. The Department of Children and Family are notified and become involved for the first time.

At the age of fifteen, Biannela leaves her toddler in the care of his thirty-four-year-old grandmother, Sonia Valdez, as she is invited over for her first real sleepover with a girlfriend. However, instead of providing proper care for her two-and-a-half-year-old grandson, Cristian is found at 4 a.m. wandering around a South Florida motel parking lot close to a busy road. He is filthy, naked, and hungry. Sonia is tracked down living in squalor in one of the motel rooms. When they find her, she is drunk and has cocaine in her purse. In a corner is a baby bottle crawling with worms. Sonia is subsequently charged with child neglect and drug possession.

Cristian is placed with his maternal step-grandfather, who promptly returns him to his grandmother, Sonia Valdez, as soon as she is released from jail.

The following year, on March 19, 2002, the Department of Children and Family investigates the family again. This time the baby is living with his grandmother and mother in a trailer in deplorable conditions. The mobile home has no electricity and no water. Biannela stays at home with her three-year-old toddler day and night, while Sonia is largely absent getting high. Finally, someone notices the situation and contacts the police.

Cristian is removed from the home and enters a foster home at age three. While there, he is assessed and diagnosed with a severe receptive/expressive language and speech disorder. He is classified as Specific Learning Disabled and Language Impaired in pre-school.

At age four, when Cristian is assessed in pre-Kindergarten, he scores above average on IQ testing. However, despite this, he is more than a year delayed in receptive language and a year delayed in expressive language. He scores high on inattentiveness, hyperactivity, and oppositional behaviors. Again, he is diagnosed as being Language Impaired, Learning Disabled. Spanish as a home language is noted.

At some stage during this period, Biannela's mother is deported back to the Dominican Republic.

At the foster home, young Cristian shares a room with two other boys. While he is there, Biannela walks into the room and witnesses an emotionally disturbed six-year-old foster brother molesting her son.

After this incident, Biannela successfully demands to be placed in the same foster care home where she can be with her baby and keep him safe. It is here she has the opportunity to carry on with her education, improve her parenting skills, and is provided with other coping mechanisms needed as a single mother from a dysfunctional home.

She moves Cristian into her own room and takes him to therapy after the sexual abuse incident. When he starts kindergarten, she chaperones all his field trips. She enjoys being a mother.

However, the stability does not last. When Cristian is four, he witnesses their foster mother dying of a heart attack at home. Cristian, Biannela, and the two foster brothers are moved to the foster mother's sister-in-law's home.

After a while, Biannela gets a job as a cashier at the fast food restaurant chain KFC (Kentucky Fried Chicken) and starts saving $200 a month. She enrolls in a program to try to obtain her GED (General Equivalency Diploma) but is unable to accomplish this goal as she struggles to juggle work and studying.

"Biannela is a very caring mom but needs to be more stern," writes a foster care counselor after an assessment of Biannela. Somehow, she is functioning as a mom but a psychologist's assessment comes with a warning: "She has difficulty making decisions. She is easily overwhelmed emotionally. She is also prone to spend much time ruminating about a situation."

By the time Biannela turns eighteen she has

saved enough money to move herself and five-year-old Cristian into their own place. They are noted as being, 'very close'. She buys an old Toyota and teaches herself to drive. She makes Cristian a promise: he will never go back to foster care again.

It is about this time she meets Luis Alfonso Galarraga-Blanco. At first, he is very attentive and is the first person to buy Biannela flowers. On their first meeting, he gives Cristian candy. She is smitten. Born in Miranda, Venezuela, December 29, 1979, Luis is seven years her senior, a former minor-league baseball player in his home country, and a construction worker by trade.

Biannela will soon learn, despite his outward charm, that Luis Galarraga-Blanco is not only work-shy but also abusive. With a heated temper, it will not be long before he lashes out at her and Cristian, both physically and psychologically.

Just after Cristian's sixth birthday, his pregnant eighteen-year-old mother marries twenty-six-year-old Luis Galarraga. Over the next five years, between the ages of nineteen and twenty-three, his mother gives birth to three children. She has a son, L.G., a daughter, L., and David, born August 14, 2008.

Cristian's world is shattered. For years he was an only child, never having to share his mother with anybody, not a sibling, not a spouse. Now he has a stepfather and three half-siblings. He finds it difficult to adjust. While living with Luis, he is distressed when he witnesses his mother repeatedly subjected to domestic violence at the hands of this new man in her life.

When Cristian is eight years old, the Department of Children and Families investigates a report in 2007 that Cristian is being sexually molested by his twelve-year-old cousin. Officials are aware of some disturbing behavior the young boy is exhibiting. Psychological reports note he kills a pet kitten that scratches his face by punching it and slamming its head on the floor. He masturbates at school. Another incident is noted where he simulates a sex act on a male child twice his age. Authorities believe there is a problem within the home environment and they hope to establish the cause of his behavior.

Authorities hear his stepfather taunts Cristian for being gay as a result of the molestation. Such are his concerns for the boy's sexual orientation, as he perceives it, Luis encourages Biannela to send him back to the Dominican Republic for a while so he can be 'cured'. Cristian's stepfather tells Cristian he needs to be a man.

Decisions are made, and they send him to stay with Biannela's aging grandmother whom he has never met. When he comes back to Hialeah, one of Miami's metropolitan cities, a year later, he has to share the apartment with two toddlers and the new baby, David, who is almost a year old. With only two bedrooms, Cristian initially has to sleep on the couch.

Trying to keep the family together and provide economic stability, Biannela works two jobs. She has a position answering phones for a tutoring company and another where she cleans motel rooms. Luis takes care of the kids and no longer works.

Once, an elderly neighbor asks Cristian why he is always doing the laundry as she sees him constantly down at the apartment complex's washers and dryers. She recalls him saying, "Because my mom is working." She remembers him being quiet, withdrawn, but she never sees or hears he has a violent side.

Another resident tells a different story. Ivette Michelena says the boy was known to take the neighbors' clothes out of the washers and dryers and one time, even threw them over a fence. She guesses it may have been because he was under pressure from his high-tempered stepfather to get the laundry done faster.

Having seen what substance abuse did to her mother, Biannela does not take drugs nor does she drink. She just wants to be the best mother she can and give them the love and security she never had.

However, she does nothing to protect her oldest son from the continued and escalating violence against him at the hands of her husband, Luis. For the year after his return, Cristian is called derogatory names. He is slapped, punched, burned, threatened with a gun, hit with a baseball bat, and slammed against the wall on various occasions.

Early in sixth-grade, his stepfather causes bruises to his back, arms, and neck. A few weeks later, he attacks Cristian again.

This attack will start like the rest, but the fall-out will be far-reaching, and will affect all family members involved.

ABOUT THE AUTHOR

Kathryn McMaster is a true crime writer of modern day cases as well as Victorian-era crimes. With a double degree in English Literature and Psychology, and extended studies in Forensic Psychology (Criminal Investigation), she combines these interests with detailed research, to explore the dark side of the human mind. It is not the 'what' of crimes that fascinates, but rather the 'why'.

Don't miss out! Follow Ms. McMaster on her Amazon profile page so you can be notified of all her new releases.

https://www.amazon.com/Kathryn-McMaster/e/B01BQ4ZCD8/

OTHER BOOKS BY KATHRYN MCMASTER

 **Who Killed Little Johnny Gill?** – is the very successful fact-fiction debut novel by Ms. McMaster covering the heinous murder of a young Bradford boy in Victorian England, 1888. The murder is so shocking it is thought to be the work of Jack the Ripper. (***Published 2016***)

Blackmail, Sex and Lies – looks at the life and  times of the infamous socialite, Madeline Smith, accused of murdering her working-class lover in Scotland, 1856. As more of the story is revealed, questions arise as to whether Emile L'Angelier, who was an avid arsenic eater, died rather conveniently or whether he was indeed poisoned by Madeline Smith to make way for her wealthier suitor. (***Published 2017***)

Kids who Kill: Joshua Phillips (Book 1) Fourteen-year-old Josh Phillips kills his young friend and neighbor, Maddie Clifton one afternoon, in Jacksonville, Florida. He tells investigators it was an accident and that he hid her body under his waterbed for a week because he was scared of his father. However, with pornography found on his computer, is Josh Phillips as innocent as he professes to be, or is this a sex crime? (***Published 2018***)

Kids who Kill: Eric Smith (Book 2) Was the youngster who enjoyed maiming, torturing and killing small reptiles, birds, and cats a serial killer in the making? When he graduates to killing people, he shows no remorse for the murder of little Derrick Robbie, a preschooler he didn't even know. This is the chilling story of a young killer who sadistically enjoys the killing: staying with the body, playing with it, and rearranging it, long after death. (***Published November 2018***)

Kids who Kill: Cristian Fernandez (Book 3)

Twelve-year-old Cristian Fernandez of Jacksonville, Florida is indicted for killing his two-year-old half-brother. He earns the dubious title of being the youngest criminal ever prosecuted as an adult in Florida's legal history. However, there is a lot more to this story than first suggests. Is Cristian really responsible for his brother's death, or does he take the blame to protect his mother? (*Published 2018*)

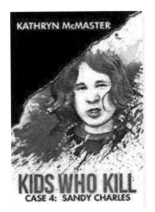

Kids who Kill: Sandy Charles (Book 4) this is not a book for the faint-hearted. It is a gruesome and senseless crime of a young boy that perhaps could have been prevented. With mental health issues and fantastical beliefs, did society fail Sandy Charles, including his own mother, or was he born just bad? (*Published February 2019*)

Kids who Kill: The Shoreline Six, Warren Glowatski & Kelly Ellard (Book 5) The book covers the murder of a young teenager, Reena Virk, killed in a swarming led by her peers and two strangers when bullying gets out of hand. Was the attack racially motivated or was it driven by Reena's desperation to be accepted by a fast crowd who would never be her friends? (***Published March 2019***)

Couples who Kill: Elytte and Miranda Barbour (Book 1) - This is a new series by Ms. McMaster that covers the death of Troy LaFerrara by the Craiglist Thrill Killers and newly-weds, Elytte and Miranda Barbour. When married Troy turns to the Internet to look for sexual favors outside his marriage, he has no idea the young girl he has agreed to meet, has very different plans for him that evening. (***Published April 2019***)

If you have enjoyed any of these books, please leave a review on Amazon and/or GoodReads, and share the book with friends & family who like to read true crime.

https://kathrynmcmaster.com/

www.truecrimepress.com

Printed in Great Britain
by Amazon

74336112R00111